"In My Staying Is Your Going"

Published by New City Press
202 Comforter Blvd.,
Hyde Park, NY 12538
www.newcitypress.com

Translated from the original Italian edition
Nel mio stare il vostro andare:
Vita e pensieri di Chiara "Luce" Badano.
© 2019 Edizioni San Paolo;
© 2019 Città Nuova Editrice.

"In My Staying Is Your Going"
The Life and Thoughts of Chiara Luce Badano

Translation by Bill Hartnett and Maria Blanc

Cover photo: Foundation Chiara Badano

Cover design and layout by Miguel Tejerina

Library of Congress Control Number: 2021943925

ISBN 978-1-56548-706-2 (paperback)
ISBN 978-1-56548-707-9 (e-book)

Chiara Badano Foundation

"In My Staying Is Your Going"

The Life and Thoughts of
Chiara Luce Badano

New City Press
Hyde Park, New York

*We have only one life
and it's worthwhile spending it well.*

Chiara Lubich

Contents

Preface

At least in my experience, God's Providence seems to surround the Focolare Movement in a particularly intense way.

This book is coming out during what I hope will be the final stages of the COVID-19 pandemic. These past two years of terrible suffering and death (particularly in Italy, which was hit the hardest of any Western country right out of the gate), have undoubtedly tested the faith of many. The "problem of evil" is one of the primary stumbling blocks for those who otherwise would likely be drawn to religious faith—and one might think that the terrible things the pandemic has wrought will make a bad problem that much worse.

But I would suggest these two years could very well lead to a religious revival. If that seems unlikely, or even a kind of paradox, the story you're about to read may challenge you.

Other than being formed by the Gen community, the Focolare youth, Chiara "Luce" Badano was very much a normal Italian teenager. One of the ways in which she was normal is that, like so many other young people in the developed West, she had started the process of losing her long-held beliefs, including her religious beliefs. The structures of Western-style individualistic consumerism were doing their secularizing work.

But then came osteosarcoma—one with the worst kinds of cancers anyone could get. Chiara knew it was almost certainly a death sentence.

Her nearly unbelievable reaction, having been trained in Focolare spirituality, was to say, "This is a chance to love Jesus Forsaken." Thus began the incredible journey of which you are about to read—a journey inspired by God's holy light shining in and through her.

By her own admission, Chiara had become "too absorbed by insignificant things, useless and passing things" but, after the diagnosis, she was pushed to abandon these things and submit to God's plan. That plan was the transformation of her own life, the lives of those around her, and the lives of those who would come after her.

The foundress of the Focolare had nicknamed this young girl "Luce" a few years prior. The name Chiara can also mean light or, perhaps more precisely, a kind of brightness which brings clarity. Somehow, impossibly, Chiara Luce radiated her joyful light throughout the process of dying. When the time came for her to pass from this life to the next, Chiara told her family: "Mamma, bye. Be happy because I am."

The abandonment of her will to God, and her connection specifically to the witness of "Jesus Forsaken", had produced in her what Pope Francis sometimes calls the joy of one who has stigmata.

And her transformation through faith into bright joy would go on to transform others, starting with her parents. Even as they were losing their only child, Chiara's father said:

> "We saw the hand of God in the illness. I
> discovered a family that I didn't realize I had.
> And Chiara's relationship with Jesus helped us

take the necessary spiritual steps ahead. Chiara
was desperately ill, and yet we never fell into
despair, because in her there was always Jesus."

Chiara also had a tremendous impact on those around
her in the hospital. She often counseled her hospital room-
mate who was dealing with depression. A hospital worker
in despair at seeing so many children with cancer every day
had "the best Christmas of [her] life" after talking for a
while with Badano. Her doctors were astonished at the way
she dealt with the disease and some of them still visit her
gravesite to honor her memory.

When she died in 1990, at the age of eighteen, more
than two thousand people from all over the world traveled
to the tiny town of Sassello, Italy, to attend her funeral. I
was fortunate enough to attend her beatification in Rome
in September of 2010, and it was a truly astonishing event.
More than 20,000 people from more than seventy countries
across five continents came full of electric, joyful energy
and clarifying light inspired by Chiara Luce. The energy
and light in these people was able to produce the kind of
unity between people one almost never sees in individualistic Western cultures. Even when they lacked a common
language to speak, they nevertheless somehow still found
ways to relate to and love each other. God's transformative
grace was clearly at work in this community of people.

And let us not forget this overarching part of the story
of Chiara's death. She was fortunate, in a way, to die within
the tightly-knit arms of a loving family and broader faith
community. Both before the pandemic, but especially during it, this is not the way many people die in our own time.

Especially in a consumerist throwaway culture, which essentially warehouses the sick and dying far away from those who find their dignity inconvenient, a key lesson of Chiara Luce's story is that God can work in surprising and even shocking ways through loving communities.

Without her formation in the Focolare community, Chiara almost certainly would never have responded to the news that she was dying by drawing closer to Jesus Forsaken. She would not have been sustained through the struggles, and she would not have had such an immediate group of people to inspire. God's Providence brought great joy and meaning (out of what otherwise looks like nothing more than a horrific tragedy) through the loving relationships of Chiara's community.

In both living and dying, let us call on the clarifying light of Chiara Luce Badano to show us the way to form and sustain loving and faithful communities. In doing so, there is no limit to the goodness and joy God's grace can bring—even in the midst of tragedy and death.

Blessed Chiara Luce Badano, pray for us.

Charles Camosy

Associate Professor of Theology at Fordham University and author of *Losing Our Dignity*

Part One

Introductions

Letter to Reader from Maria Teresa Badano

Dear Reader,

For some time, now that Ruggero has left me too, I've been feeling lonely. There is a big void in me, but in spite of everything, I feel that he and Chiara are in my heart and support me in my daily efforts and small daily problems. When the pain is stronger, I don't ask God why he took them from me, but thank him for giving them to me. I turn to them when I have to deal with difficult decisions that I sometimes must face. I feel their presence lighten my sorrows and amplify the joys. Because just as we shared everything when they were alive, so do we now, with the difference being that in place of a physical reality there is a spiritual one that is no less real.

During her illness, every now and then, Chiara would give us tasks. One day she said to me: "Mamma, when I've gone to Heaven, you'll write this experience that we've lived together and you'll share it with others." We felt that what she asked of us was beyond our ability, but she encouraged us with that same determination that she always had in life. Many years have passed since then. At the time, we did write a brief summary about our life with her, just to respond in some way to this wish of hers. I remember that when they began to invite us to go places and share our experience, we approached Bishop Maritano to let him know and to ask him what we should do. He replied: "If they invite you yes, but don't let it come from you." And from then on, that's how we've dealt with every invitation. It's what we continue to do even now, since I receive so many invitations from all over the world to bring the testimony of that extraordinary adventure that I had the gift of sharing with Chiara.

And in this I am not alone. There is Chicca—Chiara's best friend—and her brother Franz, her "biographer" with whom we share many of these joyful trips. There are many of Chiara's friends who are also giving their testimonies and helping to welcome the many pilgrims who come to Sassello almost every day. There's also the Chiara Badano Foundation that was begun at the behest of Ruggero in February 2011, a few months after her beatification, which for years has been spreading and protecting her image and memory in a thousand ways, including the official website dedicated to her. We're a squad, or better, a family, where everything happens in simplicity, in truth, in the communion of ideas, inspirations and decisions. And even after us, the Chiara Badano Foundation will remain forever, and those dearest to us will have the task of continuing the work we have begun, carrying it forward.

When Ruggero was still with me, we would often ask ourselves how Jesus could have chosen us for such a great gift as to have us spend our lives with Chiara, and we felt undeserving of the joy of seeing her proclaimed blessed by the Church. These are questions that I still ask today and the answer is always the same: It's true, God simply used our nothingness and he did everything! I thank God every day for giving us a daughter like her.

The fact is that "the Lord gave and the Lord has taken away." Of course, he asked a lot of us, since there's no greater suffering than to watch your own daughter dying in her prime. But there's no doubt that God also showered many "graces" upon our modest lives. First of all, looking back on those years, God gave us the chance to watch her grow up, to accompany her in her little discoveries as a child. Like Ruggero, I too am grateful for having been able to share with her the beauty and the concreteness of the Gospel, the belief in God's love. We accompanied her with joy—supporting her as much as we were capable, of course—through the troubles of every adolescent. And with her we discovered something new every day.

Then, the arrival of her illness, with a diagnosis so shocking that we felt like we were dying. Suddenly, our lives changed, finding new dimensions, and the relationships between us, new depths. So many times I saw our roles reverse. So much so that one day during a conversation I told her: "Chiara, now it's you who are mothering me." Little by little, Chiara taught us to transform every suffering into love. She united all her suffering to Jesus, creating the conditions for us to have Jesus' presence in our midst, giving us the strength to accept his will in the best way possible. Ruggero would say: "For our family, these two years of Chiara's illness were the most blessed by God!"

Those who don't yet know Chiara will have the opportunity, on the following pages, to learn about the main stages of her journey here on earth, to discover the intimate regions of her soul and her way of facing life. Much of it is an update, with many new details that were part of an audio-book that came out a few months ago. This text is also punctuated by many of Chiara's own words, things that she wrote or said, brief for the most part, because she preferred gestures and actions over words.

For my part, today more than ever, living for her means to always be rooted in the present moment as much as I can: without regret for the serene life we had before; without too much nostalgia, and without living only on memories. Because this life as a "threesome" continues and as I was saying, for me Chiara— and now also Ruggero— continue to guide me and the Foundation. They make their presence felt in a thousand ways and continue to be the best gift Heaven could give me.

I know that it's the same for many others in different parts of the world: just by going online— and on the website dedicated to her—they will be able to see the many wonders that Chiara's story continues to generate around the world. Chiara was a girl in love with God and life and she infected many other people with that love in those days. She continues to do the same today. She asks me to keep playing God's game, in a loving contest that makes me experience an increasingly new life.

Not that I don't miss her, obviously, just like I miss the sense of family and tenderness that until the end we shared along with Ruggero; especially during the times when I feel the weight of certain responsibilities and decisions I have to make. So, in the most difficult moments, I ask Chiara to "caress me," to help me carry on, certain of her closeness, just like I ask Ruggero to continue to support me and enlighten me with his wisdom. And every time I feel that each of them continues to do their part, often in ways and with timing that takes me by surprise.

From time to time I still wonder whether Chiara is happy with me, with my decisions and even more so with my actions. Naturally, I don't have any sure answers. The only certainty that continues to fill my heart is the one that Chiara placed inside me before she died, when Ruggero and I asked her how we were going to live without her: "Mamma, don't worry," she said, "you follow God, and then you will have done everything." And that's what I want to continue doing with all my being.

As many people know, Chiara left us saying: "Mamma, bye. Be happy because I am." Thus, now I feel that she is with me more than ever and that she asks me to continue to seek this happiness and to practice it. I'm not always able to, but each time I can't go forward—as with so many other resolutions—I feel that even in this she was right, when, along with her spiritual mother Chiara Lubich, she reminded us that the beauty of Christianity is that you can always start over.

Happy reading, and a big hug from me!

Maria Teresa Badano

Reflection of Bishop Luigi Testore, of Acqui

I have been deeply moved and impressed by this book from the Chiara Badano Foundation. I already knew Chiara's story, but when I became the bishop of her diocese I had the opportunity to read much more about her. Through this book I seem to have understood much more about the meaning of her story and the adventure she lived.

It is interesting that in this book it is mostly Chiara herself who speaks. The short quotes of what she said and wrote allow the reader to enter more deeply into her soul and spirituality. You sense the deep love that characterized her short life. You perceive the tenacity with which she faced suffering and death.

Chiara expressed a humanness capable of freeing itself from slavery, almost like a sentry who sees the dawn long before everyone else. Chiara, through her words, takes us by the hand in search of the infinite, giving us a glimpse of life's deepest meaning, because she knows how to open herself to the eternal.

It is right and important to hand on the testimony of those who knew and loved her, so that those who meet Chiara in future, without ever meeting her in person, will be able to understand the great spiritual depth that characterized her.

+ Luigi Testore

Bishop of Acqui, Italy

(Petitioner in the Cause of Canonization of Chiara Badano)

Reflection of Fr. Mirco Crivellari, Pastor of Sassello

I think that Chiara's existential journey and example cannot end in mere memories, because I am increasingly realizing that it is life. Through meetings, testimonies, prayer and sharing, I see something real blossoming, something that would never have been there if the mystery of our life and also our suffering was not connected to love.

"In my staying is your going."

"In my staying." We can understand the entire mystery of Chiara's life in this staying—her illness, her joy, her faith, and her offering. She "stayed" with Jesus, she "stayed" with the One who was Everything for her.

"Your going." That going represents a dynamic, a "producing fruit" that is possible only if the "grain of wheat falls into the earth and dies." This is real, and I can bear witness to it as the pastor of her parish in Sassello. Faces, names, stories, requests for intercessions, births, confessions . . . all unfolding in a dynamic of springtime that only the Gospel can explain. "If you remain in me and I in you, you will bear much fruit."

If you have these pages in hand, if you are about to read these testimonies, know that you will also be involved in this springtime dynamic that has to do with the mystery of God. And nothing will ever be the same:

Chiara's smile and joy will reveal to you another world, a splendid design!

Happy reading, or better, happy encounter!

Father Mirco Crivellari
Pastor of Sassello from 2012 to 2019

Reflection of Daniele Buschiazzo, Mayor of Sassello

Chiara's short but intensely real life was all in all a loving lesson. It was a call to action, a rejection of indifference: [she is] a genuine role model, especially for young people whom we hope will grow in number, despite the difficulties, and will know how to engage in welcoming and supporting their neighbor, as Chiara was able to do.

Through all her reflections, one understands that faith is a conquest (and a daily challenge) that is brightened by hope and accompanied by charity. It is not an individual conquest but rather with others, side by side, within a community that is firm in its own values and beliefs, but also open and accepting of others.

Sassello, Chiara's birthplace to which she was always very attached, is a small town where human values still count for much. Luckily, this strong sense of human values is preserved in small towns like Sassello. Each member of the community has an important role to play and is appreciated for that role. Every member of the community is important. From this communal sense comes an understanding that every person matters, and solidarity is born. It is in the "little things" that generosity and sensitivity toward others enter into the ordinary [of life]. In small towns like Sassello what is generally considered extraordinary today is still ordinary. It is normal, not only because of the natural way that such solidarity is expressed, but also because of the care and consideration with which it is practiced.

Chiara continues to give us this vision of life in a place where no one is anonymous and everyone matters, and this is the result of a daily, discreet effort that we should continue to pass on to future generations.

Daniele Buschiazzo

Mayor of Sassello since 2013

"In My Staying
Is Your Going"

Part Two

Chiara Luce Badano's Life

A Simple Family

Chiara Badano was born in Sassello, [Italy], a small town on the heights overlooking the Ligurian Riviera, on October 29, 1971.

The consumeristic exaltation of the economic *boom* was already winding down. This would soon give way to revisionist fever and the gloomy, terroristic Years of Lead, followed by years of *honey* and of extreme hedonism, in which the verb *to appear* became more important than *to be* and *to do*.

Chiara's parents, Maria Teresa and Ruggero, were simple, down-to-earth people who had waited eleven years for her to arrive. From her earliest childhood they had planted in her heart solid human values, a moral sense based on the Gospel, and a love for truth and justice.

From her earliest years, Chiara appeared to be an unusual only child. She wasn't spoiled, she loved to play with her peers, and had no trouble making friends. She enjoyed nature and sports and, of course, her beloved Sassello: a handful of houses, narrow streets, chestnut tree forests, and small amaretti factories that are a specialty of the region.

She was obviously adored by her parents and relatives. She was a mix of both parents, having her mother's outgoingness, sweetness and great faith, and her father's sobriety, sense of duty, and love for the least. She was a lively but sensible and courteous little girl, accustomed to eating everything without putting up a fuss and not at all temperamental. In many ways she was the daughter that every parent would like to have, with the parents that all children would want.

Both parents were involved in raising Chiara, relying more on love and good example than prohibitions and reproaches. Chiara nourished herself on this wise cocktail of love and firmness, adding to it her own desire for freedom and attention to her neighbor that was decidedly unusual for a child of her age, a genuine *passion,* to put it bluntly, for the needy, the weak, the marginalized—in particular, children and the elderly.

In kindergarten, after watching a documentary about poverty in the Third World, she took her favorite marker pens to the teacher's desk and said to her classmates:

> *Look here, from now on,*
> *we'll take care of them!*

She writes about those childhood days:

> *I went to kindergarten at the age of three*
> *and never cried.*
> *But when they started kicking me*
> *and bothering me, I felt a bit sad.*
> *Then Mamma taught me to defend myself*
> *and from that day on they didn't hit me anymore.*

> *When my Mamma would come get me,*
> *she saw that I was happy, and she was happy too.*
> *I was a lively child.*
> *I still am now that I'm grown;*
> *the teacher always says so.*

On April 14, 1979, she writes:

Holy Week
reminds us of the passion and death of Jesus,
so we should be good and pray during this week.
Yesterday I went to the service
of the Holy 'Stairs',
and in the past few days I have been good,
so Jesus will bless me from Heaven.

When she received her First Holy Communion, the pastor, Father Bazzano, gave her a small copy of the Gospels. From that moment on, it became her favorite reading and her inseparable travelling companion.

She came to understand that those simple phrases and those parables were not fairy tales, nor mere opportunities for more or less profound or stimulating thought. With simplicity and the elementary logic of all children, Chiara realized that those pages were a sort of guidebook that was able to give real meaning to her life. But one particular encounter cemented that conviction.

When Chiara was little more than nine years old, she met the Focolare Movement. The Focolare was founded by Chiara Lubich in Trent, Italy, during the Second World War. The Movement had already spread all over the world and included members of all ages, vocations, social classes, cultures and religions.

Along with Chicca, who soon would become Chiara's best friend, Chiara begins to share in the spirituality of the Focolare Movement, which is founded on two basic principles: universal unity as the ideal and destiny of humankind, and the path to that goal: a privileged and unconditional love for God who is reduced to zero, in apparent failure who, just before dying, cried out from the Cross: "My God, my God, why have you abandoned me?"

But other aspects [of Chiara Lubich's charism] also fascinated the young Chiara Badano, such as the Marian model it follows, the possibility of making the presence of Jesus palpable in our world, and the centrality of the Eucharist as essential nourishment to help us get through each day. Chiara's encounter with the Focolare was *the* turning point in her life.

In 1980, after her first meeting with the Gen3 (Focolare members between the ages of nine and eighteen), Chiara wrote to the Focolare foundress:

We've begun our adventure:
doing God's will in the present moment.
With the Gospel in hand we will do great things!

The friendship with Chicca, who was a little older than Chiara, grew stronger and deeper each day. It was nourished by a mutual understanding and quite a few common interests: love for the sea and swimming, music and dance. They spent as much time together as they could, not only playing and having fun, but also attending Focolare events. Moreover, they shared all the joys, hopes, and problems of their young souls.

On Christmas 1982, Chiara writes:

Each of us is called upon
to prepare the way for Jesus

who would like to enter our lives, our families.
United together, we can commit ourselves
to welcome Him,
to love Him, to be no longer us but Him-in-us,
To help Him to create on earth
the new city, the city of God.

Chiara was a Gen3 and her parents soon joined the large family of the Movement as *Volunteers*[1] which gave them a further opportunity to apply the concreteness of the Gospel at home and as part of a vast universal family that was an anticipation of the united world that Chiara Lubich foresaw as the future of humanity.

In March of 1983, Chiara attended a meeting and recounted:

I got there a little tired and I
couldn't wait to go to sleep.

But when I went to my room,
there was no bed.
I wanted to get angry, but understood
that if everything had gone well,
I wouldn't have had the chance to love Jesus.
And so I was happy.

---

1. The Volunteers of God is a branch of the Focolare Movement composed of men and women who freely choose to follow God in a radical way in the midst of society.

At another meeting that year she understood that she should:

Love the people I don't like.

On June 17, 1983, at her first Gen3 Congress, in Castelli Romani, Italy, together with many other girls from around the world, she grabbed a pen and paper and wrote to Chiara Lubich:

*This was the first Congress for me
and, I must say, it was a wonderful experience.
I have rediscovered Jesus Forsaken in a special way.
I felt him in every neighbor that passes me by.
This year I have committed to see Jesus Forsaken as my
Spouse
and welcome him with joy
and especially with as much love as possible.
Chiara, I have no words to thank you,
but I know I owe everything to you and to God.*

Chicca recalls: "I think that a video of Chiara Lubich that was shown to us when we were still little kids was a turning point for Chiaretta [as Chiara Luce was affectionately called]. At a certain point Chiara Lubich opened her heart as she answered a question from some of the Gen. She confided her secret to us: Jesus Forsaken. And she invited everyone who wanted to choose Him as the 'first spouse' of their lives, to raise their hands. And Chiaretta did it, like I and many others—right away, with a momentum that

I can still feel today. That's when Lubich's famous statement: 'I have only one spouse on this earth, Jesus crucified and forsaken' became for Chiaretta the definitive love of her life. That love came before every other love, even before an eventual marriage. It was an ongoing embrace, a search for Him in every suffering of one's own life and in the life of one's neighbor."

On November 27, 1983, she wrote to Chiara Lubich:

Dear Mother,
I'm a Gen3 from Genoa and I'm 12 years old.
First of all I want to say THANK YOU from the bottom of
my heart. . .
[. . .] I rediscovered Jesus Forsaken.
At first I loved him rather superficially
and I accepted him in expectation of the joy
that would come to me. . .
I realized that I was doing it all wrong.
I shouldn't have instrumentalized Him,
but loved Him and that's all.
I discovered that Jesus Forsaken
is the key to Unity with God
and I want to choose him as my first Spouse,
Getting ready for when He comes.
Preferring Him!
I realized that I can find him in people who seem
far from God,
in the atheists,

and that I should love them in a very special way,
without any ulterior motives.
Thank you so much for everything. . .!
P.S. Would you give me a new name
and Word of Life??!!?

It was almost prophetic the way the new name would take seven years to arrive along with the Word of Life to guide her on her spiritual journey. But it would come just at the right moment, that decisive moment in Chiara's life, as we shall soon see.

Meanwhile, life continued between school commitments and life with the Gen, family and friends. October 16, 1985, was her parents' twenty-fifth wedding anniversary. For the occasion she wrote and then read some petitions during the Mass. In one petition she asks:

Jesus, make us love one another so much on this earth,
that we will reach you and be happy together forever.

Another letter of November 29 shows the remarkable growth that was taking place in her soul:

I discovered the Gospel in a new light.
I realized that I wasn't an authentic Christian,
because I didn't live it all the way.
Now I want to make this magnificent book
my only purpose in life.
I can't and don't want to remain illiterate
of such an extraordinary message.

Just as it was easy for me to learn the alphabet,
so it should be the same way with living the Gospel. . .
I discovered that sentence which says
'Give, and it will be given to you:'
I have to learn to trust Jesus more,
to believe in his immense love.

These are surprising theological intuitions for a young adolescent, but in her, as in many of her peers around the world, they seem to evade religious academies, and come to life, stripped of all the rhetoric and rendered credible by the practice.

Growing In Love

Chiara had a lot of dreams tucked away. She imagined herself married with a lot of children, travelling the world as a flight attendant, or going to Africa as a pediatrician.

She was a girl like many others, yet different. This is only one of the many oxymorons that seemed to be brought into harmony in Chiara. She was extroverted but reserved, totally feminine but with an almost masculine pragmatism and determination, a child of her times, but also able to distance herself from the trends of the times when they ran counter to her principles. With the start of high school, she was forced to face an entirely new environment. She had to leave behind the reassuring and comfortable quiet of Sassello and face all the unknowns of city life in Savona, not a huge city, but still quite scattered and chaotic.

These have been difficult days for me,
because after the move to Savona
several problems have arisen,
including school and feeling homesick for Sassello
which I was very fond of.
I understood that to be a countenance
of Jesus Forsaken.
It was difficult to say yes to him, but I tried,
starting by giving a hand
to my mother with the final arrangements.
studying my lesson because it is God's will . . .

My life was transformed.
And then the news about the Gen meetings
seemed like special help from Jesus
to always be up.

She was pretty cute, and, in spite of being reserved and not at all interested in showing off, she soon became a point of reference for many of her classmates. Chiara was the one you could confide in, the one who would listen without judging you, the trusted friend whom you could always depend on.

In the midst of the 1980s, Chiara continued in her human and spiritual growth, and if you saw her in a school photo or with friends at Gina's Coffee Bar where she would always hang out on weekends, she didn't seem any different from the people around her.

But those who spent time with her knew that there was something different about her, something that set her apart, a kind of aura that shone on anyone who passed by her. Chiara lived through one of the most glittering and boastful decades of the twentieth century, without letting herself be ensnared by any of its excessive hedonism or the fashion crazes that surrounded her. But the prevailing consumerism—material and sentimental—weighed on her . . . and the struggle became harder every day.

This month I'm finding it very hard
not to say bad words,
and even the television tempts me
with not so nice films.

Each time, I ask for special help
from Jesus to succeed.
Unity with the Gen helped me
in the more difficult moments,
to think that they too are going
against the current.

Chiara was never attracted by any particular form of radical asceticism, but she felt, ever more deeply, that she had found something better, bigger, and more durable than anything the world could offer to her or to her peers. She was genuinely in love with God, and that love blossomed in her heart and became essential and all-encompassing. But like all teenagers she began to discover that life wasn't as simple as she might have hoped.

I see the importance of "letting go"
in order to be and do God's will.
Then, again, what Saint Thérèse used to say,
that before dying by the sword,
you have to die by pinprick.
I notice that it's the little things
that I don't do well,

or else the little sufferings,
the ones that I let get away.
This is how I want to go forward:
loving all the pinpricks.

Sparks would often fly between Chiara and her father because they both had such strong personalities, but her mother would always manage to mediate and soften the tensions so that peace would return to the family, along with that welcoming warmth that everyone immediately felt when they stepped through the front door of the Badano home.

But in the fourth year of high school the situation at school plummeted. The Italian language teacher didn't care for Chiara and, despite Chiara's efforts, more and more "insufficient" marks were piling up in her progress reports. Her parents wanted her to switch schools, but she wouldn't hear of it and managed to pass by redoubling her efforts. In hindsight, maybe it wasn't the best decision, because, as the months went by, her school career became more and more of an ordeal. But no one ever heard her utter a single harsh word about that teacher.

Then again, Chiara was like that, never an out-of-place attitude, never a dirty word, meticulous but never a nerd, sociable but not at all gossipy. Some people began to call her a little nun, but it didn't worry her too much. On the contrary, in her heart, even those people were neighbors to love, along with the homeless, and the elderly in the hospice behind their house, the parish priest and teachers, the priest-haters and the holier-than-thous, the burger-joint kids and the drug addicts. In all of them Chiara tried to see and love Jesus. And to someone who told her she was deluded, Chiara said dryly:

I've never seen God either, but I see him in you!

Despite her efforts, she failed that school year. It matters little whether it was unjust, as most witnesses say today. It was a huge blow for Chiara, probably the first real drama of her life. It was accompanied by another hard blow: her first real love story with a boy, which faded away before it ever had a chance to blossom.

These are common sources of sorrow and anxiety for any adolescent who is trying to find her place in the world. The difference between Chiara and many of her peers was that she knew what to do with all those large and small sufferings. She embraced them in union with the Crucified and Forsaken God who had now become the essential point of reference in her life.

In July 1986, she wrote to a friend:

> *As you will have heard, I failed*
> *and it was really a big suffering for me.*
> *I didn't really manage to give this suffering to Jesus right*
> *away.*
> *I took a long time to get back up and, still now, when I think*
> *about it,*
> *I start to cry a little.*
> *It's Jesus Forsaken!*

Just like her namesake forty years earlier, Chiaretta sensed that the essence of love must have been found right there in Jesus Forsaken, and that "revelation" completely overwhelmed her, so much so, that she would decide to spend the rest of her life responding to that Love with her own love.

Chiara shared everything with the other Gen, even her darkness. She didn't care about becoming rich or famous, and rejected the models that were presented to her in the media. Besides, she watched very little TV, rarely went to the cinema, and even less to the disco. Neither was she very drawn to shopping or to going for a walk downtown. She preferred to be diving among the waves at the beach in Albissola, or hunting for mushrooms with her father, or going with her friends from Sassello for a hike in the woods. She also enjoyed her favorite sports when she had time off from schoolwork: she played tennis and went roller skating at a rink near her home.

She continued to imagine herself in a future filled with opportunities and happiness, trusting more than ever in the God whom she was learning to know not only in the interior sufferings, but also in the external sufferings of everyday life. And yet Chiara didn't reveal any of this to her friends. One day she confided to her mother:

I don't have to talk about God, I have to give God. . .
first and foremost by placing myself in a position
of listening,
by the way I dress, but above all
by the way I love them.

For Chiara, life was a Holy Journey, as Chiara Lubich had said, a pilgrimage to be taken up in company with others, passing through different stages, striving to make the profane sacred, and the spiritual tangible. In this journey, there are not people or situations that are more important than others. There is only what she, like her spiritual mother, called God's will, what God lovingly desired for her, and her own effort to love always, immediately, with joy—everyone and everywhere.

But there were also things that she had a difficult time putting up with, such as superficiality, gossip, social injustice and pulling back when it was time to defend one's beliefs, whether at home, in school, or among friends. One day, she raised her voice during a conversation with her father, so her mother touched her foot under the table, inviting her to stay calm, but Chiara blurted out:

And you don't touch my foot.
You're the one who taught me to tell the truth.

Her bedroom in Savona was also different from the bedrooms of her peers. Hers was orderly and rather stark, without posters of the latest divas hanging all over the walls. It had her beloved stuffed animals sitting on some shelves with a few books, her tennis racket, and the roller skates she adored. She was equally sober in the way she dressed, never looking scruffy or sloppy. She was never motivated by vanity, but by love and respect for the people whom she would meet. When her mother wanted to buy her some new clothes, she replied:

No need, I go to school neat and clean
and that's enough.

Chiara was becoming a young woman and had her own clear idea about femininity, as well. Her model was Mary, who represented a manner of being and presenting oneself that was made of a simplicity and a gracefulness that was never provocative or seductive, but charming and appealing. This could also be seen in the way she was able to adapt to any context, while remaining herself. At the same time, she was developing even more that attention for the least among us and for the broader problems of the world that she had carried in her heart since her early childhood:

I read a magazine about the Missions,
and I was struck by this sentence:
"We need to wake up! We need to commit ourselves,
each of us needs to contribute
to eliminating hunger in the world."
This is the kind of love that God wants from us
when it comes to the poor!

And the same also applied to those closest to her, her parents, of course, and also her beloved grandparents. They also provided opportunities for her to choose God in her neighbors, as Chiara Lubich had taught:

I have a paralyzed grandmother [. . .]
One day, I was asked
to go and see her more often.
And so I did.
Every day, after school, I went to visit her.
As I felt tired climbing the steps, I would say:
"For you, Jesus."

My grandma was so happy to see me
and thanked me every time.
When I walked home I felt such a huge joy
and there I realized that if I hadn't gone,
I would never have experienced anything like it!

Simple, natural, full of life and more eager than ever to face life—that was Chiara at the end of 1980. She was totally unaware of what was waiting for her right around the corner, a totally unexpected and very arduous ascent.

What You Never Expect

Without proclamations, crusades, or fanaticism, young Chiara continued to face the routines and inevitable ups and downs of daily life as a teenager with one clear goal in mind: to be an authentic and full-time Christian. She liked to turn clichés on their heads. Where appearance ruled, she pursued substance. Rather than adoring the winners, she fell in love with the losers. Where the world rewarded sensationalists and talkers, she chose minimalism and the concreteness of facts.

Life proceeded normally but something was changing in Chiara. Like most of her peers, she, too, was not impervious that she could escape the classic adolescent crises. Many of her long-held beliefs—even religious ones—began to waiver under the pressure of life's tangles. Her smile wasn't as bright. She was losing some of her self-confidence and was afraid of losing that golden thread of God's providential care that had always seemed to guide and accompany her journey. Until something totally unexpected and far more terrible upset her life completely—osteosarcoma, one of the most painful and relentless forms of cancer.

In early March 1989, she wrote and confided to her friend Giuliano:

I'm ok, Giuliano.
I'm ok, even though Mamma doesn't tell me
"it's nothing" anymore.'

To Luca, a friend to who confided his problems to her, she replies:

Yesterday I went to the hospital for an exam.
The nurse took me to a room and laid me
on a metal bed,
it was cold and uncomfortable.
I had nothing on
After a while a small team of doctors
came in and began to examen me.
I confess to you that I suffered a lot,
feeling like I was being treated like a sack of potatoes,
humiliated in my modesty,
without one word from the doctors
who only talked among themselves
with unintelligible technical terms,
heedless of my uneasiness.
I said to myself:
"This is a chance to love Jesus Forsaken,"
and then you came to my mind
and your military situation,
and I offered this difficult moment for you.

But Chiara didn't realize right away what awaited her and, at first, she saw the disease as a mere trial to overcome as she continued to love and discover, as if by magic and almost paradoxically, the enjoyment of living her youth.

Indeed, in some ways, the new adventure seemed providential to the point that she would say:

The illness came at the right time,

because maybe I would have lost myself.

It was in this frame of mind that she began her Way of the Cross that was filled with doctor visits, exams, blood tests, hospitalizations, and increasingly painful surgeries. After her first surgery, during her first visit to the oncology department, she grasped the full seriousness of her condition and, obviously, found it difficult to accept what God was asking of her. She found it hard to understand its meaning and to accept the consequences. Everything inside her was wavering and rebelling in a sort of spiritual breakdown. But the darkness only lasted for the timespan of one morning, that of March 14, 1989. After twenty-five minutes of grueling internal struggle, Chiara managed to say her *yes* to God and, from that moment on, she never looked back.

A moment later, there she was again, her usual smile more radiant than ever. She was always ready to offer everything for others.

Soon the illness had her travelling back and forth between Sassello and Turin where some friends had lent an apartment to her and her parents to spare her at least a few journeys.

This was a particularly aggressive tumor that left very little room for hope. The treatments were increasingly invasive. Chiara was often taken by fits of retching, extreme weakness, and excruciating pain. She was now living surrounded by syringes, catheters, and medicines of all sorts.

Soon, she also had to resign herself to losing her long and much loved hair. Chiara began to think that every day God was asking her to lose one thing in order to find *something else*, and each time her *yes* was amazing to people because of the firmness with which she pronounced it.

For you, Jesus.
If you want it, I want it too.

For Chiara, pain, any pain was never a curse or an enemy to be fought and probably not even an obstacle to be overcome. For her, suffering was an opportunity for her love to grow. Perhaps that is why she thought that the first sixteen years of her life had been a preparation for the last two. The illness wasn't a shift into reverse on the journey of life, but an opportunity to step on the accelerator and travel at the perfect speed.

She wrote to some friends:

I went out of your life in an instant.
Oh, how I would have wanted to stop that running train
that was taking me farther and farther away!
But I still didn't understand.
I was too absorbed by insignificant things,
useless and passing things.
Another world awaited me
and all I had to do was abandon myself.
But now I feel enveloped in an amazing plan
that is gradually revealing itself to me.

During the days of her hospitalization, there were always many people sitting outside the frosted doors of the cancer ward. Every day, Chiara sent her mother out to update them on her condition, but mostly on what her daughter was living in her soul. In this way, a sort of circle of grace was formed which lightened Chiara's pain and enlightened those who had the opportunity to share it. This, too, is—and remains after many years—a characteristic of the Gen life: to move as a rope team because it is the only way to avoid the thousands of traps of individualism, human pride, failures, and one's own inadequacy. In 1989, Chiara wrote to some focolarinas:[2]

Mindful of my own nothingness,
I try to offer my suffering
when it is most difficult,
being mindful of God's love.
I feel your unity so strongly,
your offerings, your prayers,
which permit me to jump into the Holy Journey,
and, in that way, renew my yes,
moment by moment.

After each cycle of chemotherapy, Chiara went back to her beloved Sassello. She was more and more exhausted, as

---

2. A consecrated woman member of the Focolare Movement is called a focolarina. A consecrated man member of the Focolare Movement is called a focolarino. They take vows of poverty, chastity and obedience and live in small communities of men or women called focolares, which is Italian for hearth

if her body was trying to express her complete prostration, and her eyes were expressing a union with God that seemed to overflow from some inexpressible fullness:

> *It was truly a moment of God:*
> *I was suffering a lot physically,*
> *but my soul was singing.*

Her father, Ruggero, recalls: "In the hospital, after one very painful therapy, we all managed to say how each of us lived the pain of that day in the will of God. It was such a strong moment of unity that it made her exclaim:

> *When we have this strong presence of Jesus in the midst*
> *among us,*
> *we are the happiest family in the world!"*

By May 1989, she had already lost the use of her legs and was immobilized, bedridden. Her legs were swinging uncontrollably, causing further back pain. The doctors and her parents did everything they could to relieve her pain, but it was clear that the cancer was spreading. For this reason, Chiara wanted to prepare her parents for when she would no longer be with them. On Valentine's Day 1990, she herself made reservations for them at a small restaurant and obliged them to go and celebrate, saying:

> *Stare into each other's eyes and tell each other*
> *"I love you."*
> *And don't come back before midnight.*

And to her mother:

Remember that before me, there was Papa.

Meanwhile, the world outside was in turmoil. The year 1989 was a nerve center of the twentieth century: Communism was about to collapse. In early June, the Tiananmen Square protests broke out in China. There was the collapse of the Berlin Wall, the Velvet Revolution in Prague, and the dramatic end of the Ceauşescu regime in Romania. All these events seemed to herald epochal turning points that were as substantial as those that had been triggered by the advent of the digital age and personal computers. Chiara was attentive to these events with the same hope and concern as everyone else, trying to grasp even in those events signs of God's loving plan for humanity.

On July 19 of that year, Chiara suffered some very serious internal bleeding. She could have died at any moment. The doctors, fearing a prolonged and futile treatment, put forth to Maria Teresa and Ruggero the most excruciating decision: "You tell us whether or not to continue with treatment." Understandably, torn by pain, the two of them didn't know what to say. The only thing they could do in that moment was to pray, asking God to help them understand what would be best for Chiara. In a matter of hours, that prayer spread by word of mouth among the families and young people of the Focolare Movement. Chiara united everyone beyond time and distance. It would be the oncologist, Doctor Madon, who would make the decision to go forward with treatment. That meant more transfusions and radiotherapy. A very beautiful rapport was created with the medical team. Chiara wanted to be kept informed on everything, and the medical staff brought love and gentleness to the professional care they provided to her.

One day, she gave a letter to some friends who were on their way to Lourdes:

Heavenly Mother,
certainly you will also see this tee shirt of mine,
I ask you for the miracle of my healing.
If this doesn't enter into your will,
I ask you for the strength I need to never give up.
Humbly yours, Chiara.

Her eighteenth birthday was drawing near and she would celebrate it at home. As a favor to her, the people who were treating her decided on one further session of intensive chemotherapy. But the after-effects were terrible and Chiara spent a night in atrocious pain. When she woke up, white as a ghost, she asked her mother to draw near and whispered:

I had never spent a night like that yet.
You know what, Mamma?
I didn't waste any of it, not even that much pain.
I offered all of it to Jesus!

Thus, she also overcame that umpteenth impasse and got to spend her birthday in Sassello. Chicca and the other Gen, and some friends from Turin, were there to surprise and welcome her. They presented her with a large pink hatbox.

Chiara opened it and saw a ball of fur which at first looked like a stuffed animal but was actually a small white poodle. She named it Breadcrumb and it became her most affectionate and naughty companion during her last months.

By then, there was perfect team play between her and her parents. It was hard to tell who was helping whom, and it was not easy to put into words the atmosphere that one experienced in that family. On her birthday, Papa Ruggero sent her a birthday card:

My joy,

I have so many things to tell you, but I can't tell them all to you, only a few. I apologize if I've been rude to you sometimes. I thank Jesus for sending you among us on this journey that will never end. Thank you for all the joy you have given us with your love. Thank you for having taught me how to suffer, to offer and, above all, to do God's will in the present moment. Let's continue to stay united so that Jesus will be in our midst[3]: only then will we manage, us too, with your help and His, to live in that dimension.

Closely united to you,
Your Papa.

Occasionally, Ruggero could hear Chiara humming in her bedroom. Sometimes he found himself peeking

---

3. "For where two or three are gathered in my name, there am I in the midst of them" (Matthew 18:20).

through the keyhole because he feared that his daughter would act as if she was feeling fine (so that he wouldn't feel bad) if she knew that he was watching her. But there was Chiara in her bed, smiling as always, even when she didn't know anyone was looking. And when Papa Ruggero confided to her how difficult it was for him to go along with God's will, she replied:

> *You have to break it up into little pieces, Papa:*
> *Live each minute in union with Jesus.*
> *Then there's God's grace to help you.*

"At times,"—Ruggero recalled—"I felt like a paratrooper. You jump out and you feel yourself falling, but you know that the parachute will open. That's how it was for me: At times I felt myself fall into the void, but Jesus would hear me and I had the strength to start over. There was our pain, Chiara's pains, but they were down there, they didn't touch us."

And it was the same for Chiara. She wrote to a friend:

> *Ever since my legs started going crazy,*
> *my life, as you can imagine, has changed radically;*
> *But I'm not complaining,*
> *because I know that there are people worse off than me.*
> *And then, I live in such a wonderful family.*
> *On top of that, all of my friends come to visit me*
> *or telephone me.*
> *This makes me happy and makes the time go by faster.*

But the pain granted fewer and shorter periods of respite. In one moment of particular suffering, she confided to her mother:

Jesus is using bleach to get rid of all my stains,
even the blackheads. And the bleach burns.
This way, when I arrive in Heaven
I'll be as white as snow.

Chiara tried not to waste even a minute of her time. She wrote letters, made small crafts to raise money for her beloved Africa and followed an English course on audio cassettes. Occasionally, she watched a film or the soccer matches of the World Cup on the small TV set that was placed at the foot of her bed. Sometimes she would wash vegetables for soups that were then stored in the freezer. Big and small things like that, but amazing, given the context.

Thanks to a satellite dish that was placed on the roof, she was able to follow the World Youth Day, in Santiago de Compostela, and then the Genfest, a grand worldwide celebration of the Gen Movement. She offered everything for those events and for world peace. She wanted to share everything with everyone and made herself present in a thousand ways. She also wrote to Silvana, a focolarina who was directly involved with those events:

I offer all of you my nothingness
so that the Holy Spirit
may bestow on all these young people
all His gifts of love, light and peace,

so that everyone will understand
what a free and immeasurable gift life is
and how very important
it is to live every moment of life in the fullness of God.
In my "staying" is your going.

But Africa was always in her heart too. She gave the money she received from her birthday to Gian, a friend of the family who was about to leave for Benin. She handed it to him, explaining:

I don't need this money.
I have everything!

On October 4, 1989, she sent a note to Gian:

Dear friend,
I wanted to renew our pact,
by declaring my unity for this journey of yours
that unites us in our race to holiness.
I always remember you in my prayers,
and I thank you for your own offering
which allows me to continue loving Him.
United in JF [Jesus Forsaken],
Yours, Chiara.

Most of all, she continued to offer what she was living for the myriad of people who were having problems. Chiara was convinced that all of her suffering would bear fruit for them. She writes on October 14:

Six days of therapy can seem like a few,
but for me they're endless,
because these treatments take away all my strength.
Aware of my own nothingness, I try
to offer my sufferings
in the most difficult moments, certain of God's love.

When she was able to, she would return to her schoolwork. Since the illness prevented her from attending school, in the autumn of 1989, she started to receive private lessons at home. In one essay she writes:

Let's stop for a moment to reflect on
the meaning of our lives . . .
Often, human beings do not live their life
because they are immersed in a time
that does not exist,
either in the memory or regrets of the past
or projected into the future.
In reality, the only time that anyone possesses
is the present moment, which should be
lived completely
taking full advantage of it.
By living in this way, people will feel free
because they are no longer crushed
by the anguish of the past
and worries about the future.

*Certainly, it is not easy to reach this goal
and it requires constant effort to remain in this reality. (. . .)
The only way to make the most of time
is to make sense of our every action, large or small.
A person could give meaning to everything
by going beyond selfishness
and giving value to everything
by doing it for others.
Perhaps we would have to give a new intention
to each of our actions and we would certainly feel
more fulfilled and become more aware
of the value of life as a precious gift
that cannot and should not be wasted
nor burned up in sterile selfishness
and useless ambition.*

On Christmas of 1989, she was back at the hospital in Turin. Cardinal Giovanni Saldarini stopped by while visiting the sick. When he met Chiara's gaze, he said to her: "You have a wonderful light in your eyes." After a moment of embarrassment, Chiara replied:

I try to love Jesus.

On February 22, 1990, she wrote to her friend Daniela C:

Overcoming suffering makes you FREE!!

In March 1990, she wrote to her friend, Tiziana, whose mother had just passed away:

My dearest Tiziana, hi!

First of all, I am writing to you to apologize for taking so long to write to you.
It isn't always easy
to find the right words in these
special and difficult moments.
Perhaps the best thing would be to say nothing,

but not being close to you
even with my presence,
I take this chance [. . .] to be united with you
in your and your family's pain.
These losses, especially when they are sudden,
lead everyone to reflect
on the meaning of life and of sorrow,
but if we believe in the existence of a better world,
we will surely find some comfort!
I'm sure your Mamma is in good hands!
Be brave! She will ALWAYS be next to you
from up above
and she will certainly help you [...].
Besides, you know that here in my room
you can always come.

Don't worry [...] even just to chat,
but I would be happy if you came to see me sometimes
or called me. I would come to you but . . .
Big hugs, Chiara.

Toward the Goal

Chiaretta's final summer was an ongoing escalation of both joy and sorrow. But she spent that summer focused on the present and on the people who were near to her in each present moment. One day she invited her parents to go for a rest, to spend a few hours among the greenery of the Sassello countryside. She gave her mother a book to take along and hid a note in its pages:

> *Dear Mamma, I'm right there with you!*
> *I hope you'll be able to rest*
> *and to get a tan (sun permitting!). Don't be sad.*
> *I'm happy just the same.*
> *I implore you, don't think too much about me*
> *(but a little bit yes.)*
> *But, for one day, think about the two of you.*
> *I don't know if you'll read this note,*
> *but whatever the case,*
> *I love you so much.*
> *Give Papa a kiss so he's happy*
> *(Promise? I'm counting on it.)*
> *Bye! Your Chiara.*

On July 19, 1990, she wrote again to Chiara Lubich, to update her on the situation. They had a constant and ongoing dialogue:

*I suspended the chemotherapy treatments
because it was useless to continue:
no result,
no improvement!*

Thus, medicine has laid its weapons down.

It's up to God now!

*By stopping the treatments, the back pains due to the two
operations and immobility in bed, have increased and I can
hardly turn on my hips. Tonight my heart is brimming with
joy, and you know why? I got a visit from VIR's mother (Carlo Grisolia from Genoa). It was a moment of strong J.I.M.
(Jesus in the midst). The emotion was so strong that I could
hardly speak. Clara brought me some photos of VIR so that I
could choose one, which I have here in front of me. During
the meeting with his mother, Carlo was there with us.*

*You know? His presence was so strong that at a certain point
I found myself looking at the chair to see if he was really
there? Yes, he was.
Oh Mommy, will I also manage to be faithful to J.F. and to
live to meet Him, as VIR did??*

*I feel so small and the road ahead is so difficult. I often feel
overwhelmed by the pain. But it's the spouse who comes, correct? Yes, I say it again with you:
"If you want it, Jesus, then I want it too."*

One more thing I wish to:
here, everyone is asking for a miracle
(and you know how much I want it!)
but I can't bring myself to ask for it.
I think I'm having such a hard time asking for it because
deep down I feel that it's not part of His Will.

During the same period she wrote to some friends in Loppiano:

During this period the occasions to embrace
my Spouse
have certainly never been lacking [. . .]
They're all loving occasions,
that allow me to be more rooted with you in God.

Shortly thereafter, she received the *new name* that she had asked Chiara Lubich for. And the Focolare foundress was so impressed by the radiant smile in the photo she had attached, that she wrote:

Thank you for your letter in which you send me news about your health and tell me that you had a visit from Vir's mother. The Jesus in the midst was so strong as to make you experience Vir's presence. I'm glad. Thank you as well for your photo! Your shining face expresses your love for Jesus. Don't be frightened, Chiara, to tell him your yes moment by moment. He'll give you the strength, be sure of that! I also pray for it and am always with you. God loves you immensely and wants to enter into the intimacy of your soul and make you experience droplets of Heaven. "Chiara Luce" is the name I had in mind for you. Like it? It's the light of the Ideal that conquers the world. I send it with all my love and affection.

For Chiara Badano, it was a cause for joy and certainly not a damper on living projected on others. On September 4, 1990, to a Gen whom she had known during her first hospital stay in Turin, when he was a medical student, she wrote:

Dear Ferdinando, HI!
I'd have many things to tell you, but what matters most
is to renew the presence of Jesus among us, right?
So I'm with you . . .
Thank you for the poster that you sent to me . . .
One, in Jesus Forsaken, Chiara.

Her gaze was always luminous, her attention always focused on *others,* and whoever walked into that attic bedroom was always overwhelmed by the atmosphere that could only be described as supernatural, even though, she would reproach herself:

I feel so small and the road ahead
is so hard. I often feel

overwhelmed by the pain.
But it's the Spouse who comes, correct?
Yes, I say it again with you:
If you want it, Jesus, then I want it too.

For Chiara each day was another series of present moments, each one different from the other, each one meant to be lived to the full, with the focus on whatever was being asked of her in that moment. Her heart was taken by a desire for perfection and she conveyed that desire to anyone who drew near, like Father Lino, who took Holy Communion to her every day. One morning she told him:

I'm really glad you came! All morning long I've been saying:
"Come, Lord Jesus."
And you've brought Him to me!

The same thing happened with her Gen friends and classmates, with Giuliano and the gang at Gina's Coffee Bar, with the extended family of aunts and uncles and cousins and an endless number of others. Her relationship with the Gen, even those who lived far away and couldn't visit her, was always very intense. She was living for them, and they were living for her and offering their sufferings for her.

But the tumor wouldn't stop growing. On the contrary, it was growing very quickly, but she didn't seem to be giving it any importance. Instead, she threw herself into loving.

I no longer ask Jesus to come
and take me to Heaven,
because I still want
to offer Him my pain, I want to share the Cross with him
a little longer.
Otherwise, it will seem like I don't want to suffer anymore.
He'll know when I have to leave.

It was impossible to feel compassion for her, impossible not to be jealous of her inner peace, and not to be dazzled by that joy and depth that permeated every word she said.

She spoke very little about the illness, as if it was something small that didn't matter. On the other hand, she was always interested in the troubles of everyone who went to visit her. On the feast day of Saint Claire [Santa Chiara], in August of 1990, she wrote to Chiara Lubich:

I'm with you and I offer everything, my failures,
sufferings and joys to Him,
starting over every time the Cross
makes me feel its weight.

And yet, she often felt inadequate for the task. If there was one thing she could not stand, it was being praised or admired, let alone hearing people talk about her heroism. Rather, she regretted the effort it took for her to welcome what God asked of her every day.

Well, of course, eventually I'll say it, my yes,

but it takes time.
And I'm never really sure
I've truly said it to Him!

One day, she sent these words to Adelina and her mother:

I want to ask you to forgive me because sometimes
I might have been lacking in charity toward you.

Chiara was now Chiara Luce for everyone, but Chiaretta was still herself. She very much wanted to donate her corneas which were the few members of her martyred body that still worked. And, nevertheless, she would add:

Look, I don't have anything anymore,
but I do have a heart,
and with that I can still love.

For some time, Chiara had no longer asked for anything. She simply seemed to adapt to what was happening to her.

The important thing is doing God's will.
Maybe I had plans for myself,
but God thought of this.
[. . .] You can't even imagine what
my relationship with Jesus is now [. . .]

I feel that God is asking me something more,
something greater.
Maybe I could stay in this bed for years. . .
I don't know.

I only care about doing God's Will,
doing that well, in the present moment,
keeping on playing God's game.

Her relationship with Jesus had become very intense, so intense that she often felt constrained to recollect herself for fear of losing Him. But those moments were rare. Most of the time, Chiara continued to welcome anyone who wanted to visit her, and the small telephone that was fixed to the headboard of her bed brought the whole world into their home.

"I'll be a saint if I'm a saint right now," she repeated with Chiara Lubich, while Mamma Teresa was reading one of her writings to her. It was a famous slogan of Chiara's, and when Chiaretta heard it being read with a rather sad voice, she urged her mother:

Mamma, with more enthusiasm, aye?
More gusto, more gusto!

By now, Chiara was calmly acknowledging the inevitability of her destiny, but nevertheless she refused painkillers because she felt she could aim for something greater than merely controlling the physical pain:

Morphine takes away my clarity
and all I have to offer Jesus is my suffering.

This is all that's been left to me.
If I'm not lucid, what sense does my life have?

And after yet another infusion:

Each drop can be a little bit
like the strikes of the hammer against the nails
that were used to crucify Jesus.

During those days, she made another telephone call to the Gen. It didn't feel like an imminent and heartbreaking farewell, but an invitation to carry on together:

If we were always
in this frame of mind, ready for anything,
how many signs God would send us!
[...] How many times God passes us by
and we don't even realize it!

Chiara Luce and Chicca saw each other very often. One day, Chiara asked her to sing some songs together. With the same naturalness and simplicity as always, she chose the ones that she would like for *her* Mass. It was clear that she was thinking of her funeral as a wedding celebration with the God whom she had chosen as her Spouse. And just like any other bride, she even picked out the wedding dress she would wear. She wanted it to be simple, white, perhaps with a small pink ribbon at the hips. She also sent her parents to the city of Acqui to buy clothes for themselves. She didn't leave anything to chance:

Mamma, remember:
when I come into the church, you have to sing loudly
because I'll be singing with you from there,
and pay attention to Papa, because if he starts to cry,
he'll make noise and disturb.

Naturally, not everyone understood this way of thinking and felt that it was being carried a bit to the extreme. Some people were puzzled, others were downright disturbed. But everyone agreed that this was the end, especially Chiara, who even said to her mother:

And when you dress me, you'll have to keep saying:
"Now Chiara is seeing Jesus!"

And again:

Mamma, I'd like you to put me in the ground
because in Sassello there is the custom
of enclosing bodies in the chapel walls,
And I'd like anyone who wants to come to the cemetery
and bring me a flower, even a wildflower,
to be allowed to do that.

Then her mother answered: "That will be fine, Chiara, but maybe your Papa might be a bit sad not to put you in the family chapel. And Chiara immediately replied:

Oh, no, in that case no!
If it makes Papa sad, put me in the chapel!

In the meantime, she wasn't being spared from anything, not even the torment of a spiritual trial that many in hindsight would compare to the temptations of the mystics. She would also leave that behind, finding peace of heart after yet another sleepless night. She felt the presence of Our Lady again, beside her to support her as she took her final steps.

By now, Chiara's voice had become very faint:

For now, I'm in peace.
Pray that I can stay here until the end,
And if the devil comes, I no longer fear him,
because Jesus is stronger.

She continued to prepare—especially her parents—for the moment of her *departure.* She confided to her mother:

When you want to find me, look at the sky,
find me in a small star, because I'll be there!

On September 7th, exactly one month before her death, she returned to talking about her smallness:

I really don't want you to put me up on
a pedestal . . .

> *Jesus allowed this trial,*
> *but the merit is all <u>His</u>, if I can accept it.*
> *There is very little of my own!*

She had once made a solemn pact with Chicca. The first to go to Heaven would help the other to get there. And the one left on earth would take care of filling the void left by the other. To seal the agreement, Chiara slipped a leather bracelet onto Chicca's wrist, a bracelet that Chiara had been wearing on her own wrist.

Father Lino continued to take Holy Communion to her every morning because the Eucharist gave Chiara strength to live each moment in love. One day, in a voice that was becoming more and more feeble, her mother heard Chiara repeating:

Come, Lord Jesus!

Maria Teresa still remembers that moment: "It was a moment of God. Heaven and earth seemed to be touching."

On her last day, Chiara wanted to say goodbye to the people who had come by to get news. Maria Teresa was worried that she wouldn't be up to it, but Chiara insisted. She removed the oxygen mask so that no one would feel uncomfortable. There were many people, but with just one glance she was able to communicate all the peace and serenity she had in her heart. She said goodbye to them, especially the youth to whom she felt she had to pass on her own witness and, paraphrasing Chiara Lubich, she commented:

The youth are the future. I can't run anymore,
but I would like to pass them the torch,
like at the Olympics,
where someone runs, then stops
and passes the torch to someone else:
because they have only one life,
and it's worth it to spend it well.

Her last words were for Maria Teresa and Ruggero who were by her bedside. She signaled to her mother to draw closer:

Mamma, bye. Be happy, because I am.

Those were her last words, (but not her last act of love because her corneas would be donated as she had always wanted them to be).

Chiara Luce Badano died at dawn on October 7, 1990. From early morning, there was an endless line of people waiting to pass by her bed, as well as the crowd that accompanied her to the small cemetery: the Gen boys and girls, childhood friends and schoolmates, priests, people of faith and non-believers, strangers who had met her just once or had heard about her from an acquaintance.

When Chiara arrived at the churchyard, the people stood around her coffin enveloped in a ray of sunlight as they prayed the Time-Out Prayer, a moment of silent prayer for true and lasting peace in the world. That had been a fixed appointment with Chiara every day at noon with her parents and young people from all over the world.

On this day the prayer didn't have far to go before reaching Heaven. The Word of Life that she had received from Chiara Lubich was written on her tomb: "If you remain in me and I in you, you will bear much fruit" (John 15:5). It seemed like such a poignant end of a story, but it was only the beginning of something even more wonderful.

The Adventure Continues

It seemed that everyone—her parents, relatives and friends—would have to ready themselves to carry on without her. They would have to take in their grief for the ending of a story which was beautiful, surely, but one destined to survive only in the memories of those who had lived it.

Although no one could have guessed it at the time, that's not what happened. From various places, news began to reach the local diocese and the leadership of the Focolare Movement of some more or less extraordinary events related to her story. Articles and then books began to come out, such that her bishop, Bishop Livio Maritano, who had known her personally, was convinced enough to begin the beatification process. For that occasion he wrote: "It seemed to me that her testimony was significant, especially for young people. There is a need for holiness even today. There is a need to help youth find a sense of direction, a goal, a way to overcome insecurities and solitude, bewilderment in the face of failure, suffering, death, and all their uncertainties."

"Chiara makes you fall in love," many were saying, especially young people who sometimes felt lost in a world that was often pigeonholing them into a stereotype, or looking on them as a market to be squeezed. But the youth are also the ones from every social and cultural context who have not lost the hope nor the desire to spend their lives for something more dignified and lasting than a temporary high or a career.

Alongside the beatification process, media coverage continued to increase year by year, but with discretion and none of the fanaticism which Chiaretta would surely have despised. Her first biographies were followed by songs, poems and even musicals and plays.

The long-awaited miracle also arrived. The recipient was a boy from Trieste, Italy, who in 2001 was stricken with a very serious form of fulminant bacterial meningitis. According to the doctors, he had only two more days to live. In a matter of hours, a chain of emails, messages and phone calls began, which joined many people in prayer asking for Chiara Luce Badano's intercession. Practically overnight, Andrea was completely and inexplicably healed.

Twenty years after Chiara's death, in September 2010, by decree of Pope Benedict XVI, Chiara Luce Badano was proclaimed Blessed. This took place at the Shrine of Our Lady of the Divine Love, in Rome, Italy, in the presence of more than twenty thousand people, mostly young, who had assembled from more than seventy countries from all five continents, confirming that Chiara Luce Badano was now a global phenomenon. That same evening, in a packed Paul VI Hall at the Vatican, a huge celebration was held in her honor: "Life. Love. Light." One week later, during a visit to Palermo, Italy, Pope Benedict XVI spoke about her, calling her an example of the Christian life:

> I invite you to get to know her. Her life was short, but it is an amazing message of nineteen years brimming with life, love, and faith. Two years, the last two, also full of pain, but always lived in love and in light, a light that

even radiated around her and that came from within [. . .] Chiara Badano was a ray of light for everyone.

Chiara Badano's "extraordinary ordinariness" continues to spread throughout the world like a mysterious drumbeat that doesn't seem to have a precise origin. Year by year, on the wave of her beatification, more articles, television specials, DVDs, songs and musicals have taken inspiration from her life. The world of social media, from Facebook to YouTube to Twitter, is overflowing with news about Chiara Luce. Biographies have been published in more than thirty languages (from the more familiar languages to the less known, from Korean to Croatian, from Norwegian to Turkish, from Urdu to Japanese, Armenian, Chinese, Swahili, and more). There are also projects and other initiatives that bear witness to the continuing impact of her short life. For many young people Chiara is also a sister, someone to be inspired by, a confidant with whom to establish a deep personal relationship.

As we await a new miracle to begin the canonization process, in response to the desire of her parents, the Chiara Badano Foundation continues to gather and archive everything that is happening around the world regarding Chiara Luce. The Foundation also administrates the www.chiarabadano.org website which spreads and defends her fame of holiness. Buildings of all kinds have been named after her. The first was the Chiara Luce Lodge, inaugurated in 1993. There are also countless parks, streets, gyms, oratories, youth centers, and so on. The first church building to be named after her is located in her beloved Benin. Also, in September 2015, in the presence of her parents, the first parish was inaugurated in her name in a little town in the heart of rural India. Shortly thereafter, two more churches were named for her, one in Thailand and one in Cameroon.

More so, for over ten years, her parents, accompanied by Chicca and her brother Franz, continued to travel the world, invited by dioceses, associations, schools, and prisons, to share their testimonies. They also spoke at the World Youth Day (WYD) in Madrid, Spain, in Rio de Janeiro, Brazil, and in dozens of European countries and nations around the world. They are a small squad, as Mamma Maria Teresa likes to call them, but supported by a large number of collaborators, like her friend, Giuliano, from Gina's Coffee Bar which is still a main reference point for anyone who goes to the village to visit Chiara's tomb. Not to mention the many people who coordinate and accompany visitors to the attic bedroom where Chiara spent the final months of her life, along with all those who continue to take the testimony of her parents to places they cannot get to. It is the network of Chiara's friends who now, as then, continue to rally around her memory.

On October 13, 2018, Papa Ruggero went to join his beloved Chiara in Heaven. It was a very painful loss not only for Maria Teresa, because "Rouge," as Chicca and Franz liked to call him, held an extraordinary and irreplaceable place in Chiara's story. He was a simple man, incredibly humble, who spent the final years of his life in the quiet normality of a person who did not make distinctions between watering plants in his garden and talking in front of crowds of thousands of young people. "Now I will let you go," Maria Teresa whispered to him shortly before the end. It seemed that he was waiting for that affectionate and excruciating authorization to take his leave with the serenity he had earned from a life that was paved with suffering and self-denial. "I will miss him to death," Franz Coriasco would write that day on Facebook. "I will miss his jokes, his 'mah' and his 'oh well' pronounced while shaking his white head of hair. I will miss those serious looks he put on when someone wanted to take a picture with him. I will miss his awe in front of the wonders of the world, his humility and his delightful expressions in front of a platter of cold cuts or a nice glass of red wine. Because only a man who has been able to face great tragedies in life could truly enjoy the little things. Even in this he has always been a truck driver, our Rouge, a simple man full of common sense, a man of few words—in this he was just like his daughter—but always with the right words and always at just the right moment. In a simple way, I guess, because he was *right*."

He had also dreamed of, and helped put together, this book in which Chiara Luce's words and manner would be conveyed as authentically as possible, a sort of guidebook within the reach of anyone who would like to establish a direct friendship with Chiara Luce. And all of us at the Foundation are glad that this has also come about.

Now the adventure continues for Maria Teresa and those close to her, for the Foundation and for the people all over the world who see Chiara as a sister and a guide. In other words, Chiara continues to fascinate and win over hearts everywhere. She even surprises people who never knew her.

Part Three

Testimonies

Chiara for Me...

We decided to include in this book the thoughts written by some of Chiara's friends who knew her in different ways, either up close or at a distance, during the different stages of her life, even during some of those last sharp turns in her journey. These people were the direct witnesses of her extraordinary adventure. Therefore, they are the most reliable keepers of a story that, in many cases, changed their own lives.

Giuliano Robbiano (a friend)

We lived a few steps away from each other and my memories of Chiara go all the way back to kindergarten. As teenagers we went out together with friends, taking walks, evenings at the pizzeria. Chiara was very cheerful, and she was also very cute. That's why I was always so glad when I would be at the coffee bar and she would come looking for me.

Then the illness arrived. I remember that we all spent New Year's Eve 1998–1999 at an apartment that our friends had let us use. The next morning, we had an appointment to go back and clean up the apartment, but she didn't come. We found out that they had taken her to the Pietra Ligure Hospital. When we heard the terrible diagnosis, it was a horrible moment for me, too.

Then came the chemotherapy and that wig to cover up the effects. Then she lost the use of her legs. When she told me over the phone, I felt myself dying. In the following months, I went to visit her often. She never spoke about her illness, but instead wanted to know how our friends were doing. I often feared finding myself in front of a very sad girl in need of consoling. But then, I would see her in that small room, immobile and confined to her bed, but cheerful, smiling, with her beautiful bright eyes. How she did it, I don't know; She was certainly light-years ahead of all of us in her circle.

From the beginning of the illness, we had made a pact which we kept until the end: I would telephone Chiara every day and she would let me know whether or not she could talk, or whether she wanted me to visit her. In the early days, we spent a lot of time together; whereas, in the final days, we spent hours together on the telephone.

That's how we spent those amazingly beautiful two years. I remember the time she returned to Sassello after suffering a frightful hemorrhage. "Do you know that I was supposed to die?" she informed me when I went to visit her. "Had I died, what would you have done?" The question shook me: "Chiara, you're not dead; let's talk about something else," I said with a hint of embarrassment. "No, no, answer me! Had I died, what would you have done?" She was being insistent, so I attempted an answer: "Well, I think I would do what one normally does. I would have cried, and I would have brought you some flowers." And she responded: "Well then, you haven't understood, Giuliano. Don't cry and don't bring flowers because, if God wants it, if Jesus wants it, then it's okay with me. So, don't cry and don't bring flowers."

One day, toward the end, she said to me: "I have to ask you to forgive me for something I did. I sometimes told you I wasn't feeling well but it wasn't true: The truth is that I was in a spiritual place so close to God and that to see you again meant to come down to earth, and to go back up to that place took too much effort, I just couldn't do it. But for this, Giuliano, I ask your forgiveness."

I saw Chiara for the last time in mid-September 1990. We spent a very beautiful afternoon together. She was immobile and in pain, but we "kept playing": As always, she wanted to know who was walking by on the street outside. I was a bit embarrassed to be seen looking out of that window, especially with the scarf on my head that she forced me to wear so that nobody would recognize me. I had no idea that would be the last time we would spend together.

We spoke over the phone up until the end of the month. Two days before she died, she had a note taken to me: "Half asleep, I send you my greetings and all my thanks. This is to be extended to everyone. With love, your Chiara." Every time I meet people who had become Chiara's friends in that last stage, I know that the note is also addressed to them, and I read it to them. And whenever I go to visit her at the cemetery or when I'm at home and think of her, I carry on as if she's still here; that is, we talk, we joke, we laugh. I felt a bit like I was lacking respect, because you don't joke around in front of a saint's tomb. But one time I found Chicca at the cemetery and she told me that she did the same thing, so that means it must be okay.

Tiziana Ramognini
(a friend and classmate from Sassello)

I had the great fortune, indeed, the endless gift of having known Chiara. And I shared with her and the other friends here in Sassello many joyful and lighthearted moments that were also deep, serious, and important. I attended elementary school and middle school with Chiara, and our friendship continued during our teenage years. We would get together every Saturday and Sunday at the Gina Coffee Bar, at Giuliano's, where we often spent the evenings or afternoons. We would talk, play, take beautiful long walks. There was the moment for joking and the moment for "serious things" that alternated in a natural way, as happens among friends.

Many images come to mind when I think of Chiara, some very vivid, others confused, because they were part of that period in life, adolescence, when one is inclined to run without stopping to think very often. But I know I can say with certainty that Chiara's presence and her love have never left me.

I have one very beautiful image of Chiara that stayed with me. We were around sixteen years old and I remember one evening with all of our friends. We were under the canopy at the small church of Saint Sebastian's that was one of the outposts of Most Holy Trinity Parish. We were sitting on the little wall sharing our teenage hopes and dreams. We were fantasizing about the future, and I remember Chiara's peace and determination and her endless capacity to listen, which always made you feel like the center of her thoughts.

Chiara was also a great help to me at a very painful moment in my life. In March 1990, I lost my mother to a tumor, and even though she was already so sorely tested by her own illness, two days later, Chiara managed to find the time and the strength to write me a most beautiful letter in which she encouraged me and helped me to face the pain. It was the umpteenth confirmation of how great and disinterested her love was for others, her great love and her intense spirituality.

So, the friendship that binds me to Chiara to this day is something I feel quite strongly, something that accompanies me everyday. Sometimes I feel like she's right next to me, that she gives me a little slap on the head when things aren't going well, or when I don't jump into action, or when I lose my way. And it's only thanks to her—and those who know me would agree—that I'm here right now telling you about my love for her. And even though many years have passed, each time I hear her story I tear up. Thank you again, my friend.

Glenda Badano (a cousin)

I've known Chiara since forever. We grew up together as first cousins. I've told about my bond with her on many occasions, also in preparation for the beatification, giving my testimony to the canonization process.

Our relationship changed over time: It never stayed the same: It changed and evolved over the years. But Chiara remains my strength, not only my light in the dark moments, but also my joy in the happy times. I still tell her about all my failures and successes. The happiness I feel in meeting her again is enormous. Her limpid gaze is deep inside me. I look for it, I wait for it, and when I'm in doubt and uncertain, I let it work inside me. On many occasions, it gave me the key to solving my problems, to moving on in the best way. I'm not always strong enough to follow it, to respond to all the love that it contains, but I try, I try every day."

Giorgia Badano (a cousin)

I'm six years younger than Chiara and, like many others, I also ended up on the roof of her home for one of her pranks! Out of the many memories I have of her, I often remember our escape from the "grown-ups" to go jump on our bikes and ride down the hill at Saint Anthony's Hospital. The descent was full of gravel, but she was quite reckless and this time we even ventured to try out some acrobatics on the little Graziella bicycle. She pedaled and I was standing on the luggage rack of the bicycle. I must have been five or six years old, and after the first descent I looked like poor Lazarus all bandaged up! But in the embrace of her presence, I felt like I could take any risk. How many rides we had on that mythical bike!

Ivanna Pianta (a focolarina and friend)

I got to know Chiara at a Focolare gathering in July 1981. She was nine years old. She was there with her parents who, after talking with her, entrusted her to me with a bit of hesitation. But she said goodbye to them with determination as she walked toward the other children in the group to make their acquaintance. I still remember her now, turning the corner of the building without looking back, serious and determined. During those three days together, she was cheerful and serene, deeply affected by the novel experience. Only afterwards did I learn of the apprehension her parents felt about leaving her with us, and that Chiara had tried to reassure them saying: "But Mamma, it was my choice."

This is how Chiara's adventure began with the Gen3 girls (children and teenagers of the Focolare between the ages of nine and sixteen). At the time, I was the focolarina who was entrusted with their care. Chiara began to live the charism of Chiara Lubich in her family and with the other Gen. In rereading her letters from those days, one can see how the strong experiences she had during the illness until the final encounter with Jesus were rooted in her childhood and adolescence.

Conquered by God's love, she took this very seriously and increasingly lived everything that she was receiving from Chiara Lubich and from the life of the Focolare Movement, of which she always felt a part, and in which she participated in more and more intensely, placing herself at its disposal with her many gifts and talents (of which, by the way, she never boasted). She knew how to recite and to sing, and always gave her best in so many ways, especially with Chicca. She could have become a leader, or at least feel like one, but she was never drawn to be like that.

Here, I can't neglect to mention the other Gen3 who were younger than her, because they also shared in that "adventure" with Chiara. Her exuberance when they were together was very engaging: There were moments of joking, playing, laughing, and confiding in one another, which bound the children more and more to each other. And it was with these little girls that I lived the news of the illness and all the strides that Chiara was making toward Heaven. What were my and their small sufferings in comparison to hers? So, together we offered each and every suffering for her—and we did it gladly.

In the years that I lived with Chiara, my relationship with her, the love and the sharing, grew and became stronger. A very deep relationship of mutual love was formed, with a willingness to give our life for one another, if necessary. In September 1987, I stopped being the Gen3 assistant, but continued to follow her from afar. There were fewer opportunities to see one another, but whenever we did, a simple glance was enough to understand that we were still living one for the other. That's how I spent her entire illness, at a distance, even though I was updated on a regular basis and shared the whole experience with those Gen3 who were now young teenagers and still very connected to her. I only got to visit her once during the final months. You couldn't go into her unless you were completely in God. We planned to meet in Heaven above, and in the heaven of suffering-love in every moment, here on earth. I felt so encompassed by her love.

On October 6, 1990, at around 4:30 p.m., I was at school for a meeting when I realized that I couldn't stop thinking about her, as if she was really right there next to me. I knew that since the night before she was very ill. I wasn't able to do anything but continue to follow the meeting with all my attention, with all my love for my colleagues, and I noticed a great peace in my heart. This continued at Mass and I felt a strong, inexplicable union with God. When I reached home, I learned that during that very hour, Chiara had said farewell to all the people who were there with her—also me! In God all things are possible. In the years that followed, we came to know with much amazement that on that same evening, in slightly different ways, Chiara had "passed by to say goodbye" to several of those young Gen3 who loved her so much.

Patrizia Casella (a friend)

I got to know Chiara in 1986. A special friendship began between us at the meetings for Focolare families. We were both kids and visited with each other on weekends. We took long bicycle rides, roller skated, and ate warm focaccia bread on frost-covered meadows. What struck me about her was her simplicity, her availability to everyone, and the way she acted out of personal conviction.

I came to realize that Chiara was no ordinary friend. She truly loved me and I felt very united to her. I realized that there was a life within her that went beyond the way of being and having fun of any ordinary girl that I knew.

I was immediately drawn by her way of living. I felt that just by living the ideal of God-Love our friendship would be complete; it was helping us to grow and leading us to God.

Then came the illness, a real thunderbolt in the middle of a quiet sky. I was struck by the way she faced it all and how she accepted it as a way of reaching God. In the end, her departure to Heaven happened during a very particular time of my life; Chiara was the bridge between the light and the darkness that I was living. She was my hope in life, and now God was taking her away from me. Everything could have fallen apart around me, but I felt like what I had built with her during her illness remained standing, because it had been done with love. The day of her funeral was defining for me, because I felt that I could entrust everything to her with confidence, because her love for me continued. Thanks to her, after much suffering, I found peace and serenity again.

I can also testify, after so many years from her departure, to all that Chiara has given me with her life. I do it as a way of giving thanks to God for all that God has done in her, in me and in spite of me, and for this most precious gift of her friendship both on earth and in Heaven. Forevermore!

Giovanni Giuseppe Amoretti
(Chiara's high school teacher)

Laura B; Ilaria C; Simona D; Paolo I; Daniela L; Alessandro M; Alessandra M; Fabio M; Luca N; Tullia P; Debora P; Tiziana R; Angelo R; Francesca S; Laura B.: Chiara's classmates, names and faces that continue to fill the memory and the heart of Chiara's elderly high school teacher.

Nearly thirty years have gone by and the shadow of time has settled on the faces of those alumni, but their eyes still shine with the light of youth. Among them, with them, Chiara Badano also smiles today—Blessed Chiara "Luce" Badano. Her gaze lingers on each one of us, her hand hints at an affectionate goodbye.

You went away just like that, on a faraway autumn day, leaving an empty seat, your classmates and teachers all heartbroken, but setting a path for us all, which leads from suffering to love, from the suffering of our dying bodies to the peace of Jesus Christ. Igniting Christian hope in the hearts of all who love you.

Simona Damonte (a high school classmate)

A clear day, the warm sun, the scent of the ocean breeze, a happy feeling, an encouraging push, a listening presence that understands—Chiara is this and much more.

She is the smiling girl who dialogues with everyone. In her I hold all my memories of school: her smile; conversations with everyone, without distinction, and not just to be more empathetic; the courage she demonstrated in confronting two particularly harsh teachers; the joy that she let explode during the few minutes of recreation in order to free her mind and breathe in a few moments of lightheartedness.

Unfortunately, I was merely a spectator, because I didn't possess her strength of mind and didn't know how to feel the same joy: I was closed in my dark shell, which made it impossible—on my part—to share in those moments. But if I think back to Chiara, to those episodes and to my current life, I can say that they are numerous the opportunities I now have to offer to adolescents who find themselves in dark shells today, that which I learned slowly and reflected upon over time: remembering, reflecting, listening with the heart as well as the mind—strength and serenity for a generation of youth made of contradictions, fears and much fragility which, as it turns out, is not much different from our own. I don't speak explicitly about Chiara with them, but I do ask myself what she would say or do in this or that situation. Then I let my heart speak.

I believe that I am not wrong in saying that she feels nearer to me now than she did back in high school because I've changed: I've removed my shell and made room for her words, both spoken and unspoken. I can no longer listen with my ears, but I have fixed in my mind the joyful sound of Chiara's voice speaking to me over the phone as she lay on her bed of pain: This is not the voice of a person saddened by her illness, but happy because of life.

At her departure, we— classmates, teachers and friends—were asked to write a few lines as a memorial. In mine, about halfway through, I wrote that I have to put into practice what she taught me. I can truthfully say that despite my being just a drop in the ocean compared to her, I keep her example in mind, especially with regards to my work, my family, and my social life, always aware of the fact that Chiara is right here next to me.

Daniela Lorenzini (a high school classmate)

A few weeks after her departure for Heaven, I had this dream: I was on a bus that I often took to Mass. It stopped and she got on. She was holding her little dog Breadcrumb in her arms. And when I looked at her, I felt an overwhelming happiness inside me. We began to talk and it was nice to be with her again! A few minutes later she walked over to the bus door and said: "I have to get off here, but you have to go on."

When Chiara left us, it wasn't easy for me to accept it. I was only eighteen years old, but I think that separating from the people we love is difficult at any age. For a while, I lost faith: This God who was so insensitive to our prayers, I just didn't understand; on the contrary, I deeply hated him.

During that period, I did a lot of foolish things and made a lot of wrong choices. I lived without ever feeling at peace with myself. I thought often of Chiara, and it made me so angry I would rebel, because I didn't like that "design" [of God]. It was just incomprehensible to me. The only moments of any light and peace were when I went to visit her parents in Sassello. I naively thought that I was comforting them, but little by little, I realized that I was the one being comforted.

In one of her letters, Chiara had sent me a poem, a text by Hikmet titled *The Most Beautiful Sea*. The last few lines, in particular, read: "And the most beautiful words I wanted to tell you/I haven't said yet." Those words kept coming back to my mind and I felt that they were more than mere words, that they contained a message which Chiara had left me for my life. So, thinking about those words, I began to silence myself, to go to Mass every day. I tried to let her fall deep inside me and, ever since then, I never stopped.

Now, Chiara is my center of gravity. Every time I lose my peace or don't manage to distinguish between good and evil, I've learned to stop, as if I were driving inside a roundabout and didn't know which road to take. I try to understand which one she would consider the most beautiful from her vantage point in Heaven. Then I remember that I have to go on and everything becomes clear.

After her first surgery, she went back to school just for one day, for what I so much hoped would be a new beginning for her. Instead that would be her last day of school. She wanted to go upstairs to say hello to the teachers, and she asked me to accompany her. While climbing the stairwell that connected the two floors, she asked me for my hand and without thinking I gave it to her. I sensed that she was frightened, because I could feel that her legs were shaking (soon she would not be walking anymore), but she didn't say a word. Now, whenever I'm afraid of not making it, I remember that moment and I feel that she's still holding on tight to my hand from up there in Heaven, waiting to be able to embrace me again someday. God makes himself present in our life in many ways, through little things, simple gestures which we hardly notice but which Chiara always knew how to grasp, and I thank her for teaching me this attention to the details. One falls, gets up, and the journey begins again: this is life, what she called "God's game." I hope I have the same strength to never give up, and I know that her help will never fail me.

Caterina Varetto Coriasco
(a friend of the family)

We had a big connection with the Badanos, but with Chiara Luce's illness that bond became much closer. I remember that I often drove up to Sassello in our dilapidated little Fiat 500 just to share in any way that I could. Sometimes I just helped out around the house, like so many others. Of course, it was love from the heart that pushed me, but it wasn't an effort or sacrifice—not at all. Indeed, it felt like the most natural thing in the world. Well, that love remained even after Chiara's death (when she left, I began to entrust many complicated and painful situations to her). It remained in me as something luminous that even today warms and brightens my heart at the very thought of it. I remember when Chiaretta, through Chicca, asked me to make her wedding dress for her final walk down the aisle. She wanted it as simple as she was, and so, with the help of my sister, we made it for her with all the care that should be shown to a newlywed who is about to join herself to the love of her life forever.

Now that she finds herself among the most powerful in Heaven, I feel that our bond has deepened and become a fixed point, and she's a bit like a shoulder that I can lean on in all the difficult moments, with every obstacle that I encounter within me and in others. And one of the most beautiful things is being able, now and then, to communicate to others what we lived together, our family and hers, to tell about her amazing experience and about everything we shared over the years—from when we first met her as a small child until her departure—and also the years that followed.

All of this makes me feel endless gratitude for the gift that was given to me in being able to share in this amazing adventure. And it's the same for my husband, Michele. So, one more time: Thank you, Chiara Luce!

Aldina Bignone (a friend of the family)

Only now, after so many years, do I realize—at least a little bit—what filled the atmosphere that we breathed in at the Badano home during those years. Everything seemed so simple and even the illness was just part of life. Christianity was alive, the Gospel in action, mixed into a normal family life that was apparently like so many others.

Now, I cannot picture Chiara without Mamma Teresa and Ruggero, her father, who has recently gone to join her: The two of them lived the time of the illness selflessly, and like Chiara, lived one for the other. They were light and they contributed to making her be light.

Thus a special love was established in that family, a unity of will and of intention, of merit and of heart, where everything became possible, illuminating every moment, every suffering, every decision.

But when this occurs, it demonstrates an apparent absurdity, which some have called a "miracle": The heart can hold contemporaneously contradictory realities, a unity of opposites in which suffering and peace, suffering and joy, can coexist.

For me, Chiara was all of this, a living witness of love. It makes me think of what is written in the Gospel, that Jesus has promised no less (Cf. Matthew 18:20).

Gianfranco Piccardo (a friend of the family)

In 1989, I was offered a job in Africa to follow the construction of thirty water wells that would supply safe drinking water. On October 10th of that year, I left for Benin, not without some doubts about whether or not I would accept the job. Three weeks before leaving, I went to visit Chiara in Sassello. I had a nice relationship with her parents and I knew she was seriously ill. On that occasion, we made a pact with each other: I would offer up for her the difficulties I would face in Africa and she would offer up her sufferings for me. It was a powerful pact that I have always kept. I felt close to her and she was of great spiritual help to me. The experience in Benin was very rough. There was a military dictatorship, a lot of poverty, and no social services. I immediately thought of returning to Italy. Then, little by little, I convinced myself to stay and I think that the strength to do that came from Chiara. That pact we made was always very present. I spoke of it especially to the African children and the young people whom I gradually came to know. They were interested in her and in her story.

I stayed in Benin for four months, a stay that was interrupted with a few trips to Italy. During one of my returns, I remember going to Sassello to see Chiara. I brought along some picture slides and told her about my experiences. I could see that she was very touched by the images of the children and by what I was telling her. At a certain point in the slide-show I remember hearing Chiara ask her mother to bring her an envelope. It contained the money that she had received for her eighteenth birthday, and the sum was approximately $1,300.00. Chiara told her mother that she wanted to give that money to the children in Africa, which made her mother ask: "But, Chiara, all of it?" And Chiara [responded]: "All of it! I don't need this money, because I have everything!" I took that money with me to Africa and gave it to the local bishop.

I returned to Africa other times. One day, after Chiara's death, I went to the Badano's house. They told me that they had found a box which I had given to Chiara. It now contained a sum of money and a note that said "For Africa". Maria Teresa and Ruggero understood it to mean that Chiara intended to send more money to the children of Africa, so they began a fundraiser that continues until this day!

As such, our dialogue continues, and my remembrance of her. For example, one day, in one of the many Ligurian villages where I sometimes happened to be on business, I saw a plant with very compact leaves that resembled an agave plant, but much, much smaller. It stood there, on the tip of a fence post. I went to have a closer look and it was obvious that the plant had been there for a long time, but it had no pot, no soil. It had lived there for years, hanging from that fence post, unrooted. There are little plants like this everywhere; I even took one home and, over time, I divided it again and again—and the plant continues to grow and develop, hanging on that wall, on that stake, on that branch. And every time I look at it, I think of Chiaretta, because she wasn't rooted in the soil of this earth either.

Lorenzo Ceribelli (a friend and focolarino)

Twenty-eight years have passed since the day Chiara physically left us, but it has always been clear that the experience she made us live in those twenty months could never end. Each encounter with her was so special, extraordinary, and unique, but at the same time it was simple, ordinary, and "normal." It takes two hours to travel by car from Turin to Sassello. I used the drive there to prepare myself to see her, shaking off the "dust" in order to be ready for contact with the "Light" [Luce]. The return trip was needed to "digest" what had occurred [during my visit with her] in her little room. Then I would slowly, slowly return to everyday life.

After the two hours of preparation, upon entering her room, it would feel like there was no ceiling, and Heaven and earth had become one. How many trips and how many moments of "heaven" with her, even though every time we left for Sassello we were never certain of being able to see Chiara in person because everything depended on her physical condition. However, the encounter with her parents and the community was also an encounter with Chiara, because they were deeply living that extraordinary experience with her and with each other.

What did those nearly two years leave inside me? I remained the same as before, but with the certainty that holiness is truly within the reach of everyone and that if we respond to God's grace as she did, we can all become saints. After those famous twenty-five minutes, Chiara put her hand to the plow and never looked back. And she involved all of us, dragging us along in that divine experience.

Valerio Lode Ciprì (at the time, a member of the Gen Rosso musical group)

In the winter of 1989, we were in Turin, Italy, for a series of very packed shows. A focolarina named Paola had informed us of a Gen from Sassello who would have liked to attend the concert but couldn't because she was being hospitalized for a very serious illness. So, we said to each other, if she can't come to us, then we'll go to her! And so we took off with a few members of the group and headed with our guitar to the Molinette Hospital. When Chiara saw us walk through the doorway, she was shocked and delighted at the same time. I can still see that smile with which she welcomed us: It was already a smile from Heaven, with an incredible purity that shone through her eyes. It seemed as if, in that moment, her illness did not matter. We were there for her and she welcomed this visit as a gift, a personal gift of love from God to her.

Then we began our little improvised concert, choosing from among our "softer" music so as not to upset the hospital staff. She asked us to sing *Infinito* and the refrain seemed to have been written just for her:

In the infinity of the heavens my life/is a path of light, a clear and shining star, a moment of suffering and love/In the infinity of Heaven my life soars/toward the heights/I can't but sing and sing to Love.

She watched us in amazement and disbelief—a small concert just for her! We didn't want to tire her, so, after we made a pact with her to pray for one another, she bid us goodbye and we returned to the theater, carrying within our hearts a sense of indescribable beauty.

A few months later, she wrote to us from Sassello: "Dearest focolarini, First of all I thank you infinitely for the gift of your visit to me when I was in hospital. It was a moment of God. I remember each one of you and the grace of that day is still with me now. Let's stay united. I'm with you." Thus began a very beautiful relationship with her and we sent her a postcard from every place we performed.

That year, I remember, we received an invitation to perform in the then Soviet Union. It was almost a miracle because even though the Berlin Wall had just fallen, it was still incredibly difficult to go to the USSR, especially for a musical group that sang Christian songs. In the midst of all the bureaucratic obstacles pertaining to obtaining entry visas for people from so many countries, I recalled the pact we had made. I telephoned her and asked for help with her prayers and offering. Her response to my request was striking: "Don't worry, I'll take care of it!" With what certainty and determination did she speak those words to me, like a person who knows she can get it done, who has the faith to obtain the grace she asks for! Shortly after, I received news that it would be possible for us to go. I telephoned her right away: "I knew it! I knew it!" she exclaimed, expressing all her happiness for this "grace" that had been granted to her from Heaven, which she was quite familiar with by then. Shortly before we left, Chiara Luce flew off to Heaven. Some of us managed to go to her funeral. Afterwards, at Maria Teresa and Ruggero's house, I sang a song that I had adapted during the night for their Chiara, *God Loves Me!* I think it was the first song that was ever written about her.

I don't know how long it was after our return from that tour that I found a small envelope on my desk, containing an even smaller notepad paper. It was from her. Perhaps she had given it to someone a long time before and they had forgotten it somewhere. It had no date on it. It really seemed like a message sent from Heaven: "Hi! I'm with you! Let's continue together. The things to tell you would be infinite, but let's redeclare our desire to have J.I.M (Jesus in our midst). I think that says it all. One, Your little sister, Chiara Luce." A more powerful and encouraging message and promise could not have arrived for us. Yes, Chiara Luce, you're always with us! Let's continue together!

Marita Vignola (a friend)

Chiara for me . . . For me Chiara was a playmate, an 'untethered nutcase' on her roller skates, a beautiful human being, simple, harmonious, always attentive to the neighbor who was passing by, never making distinctions or setting limits, even in the smallest and simplest things.

At play, for example, she was really good and quite active. She was never domineering. She made room for others, even the less capable people like me, for example, who was a total failure on skates.

I disliked living so far away from her, with the thousand complications involved in getting to her by public transportation and not yet having a driver's license. It prevented me from spending much time with her. But despite the distance, she was always close to me and we shared a lot of things with each other. For example, we prayed when I was looking for work (which didn't take long then to find).

I remember the birthdays we celebrated with one another. She was born on October 29th, and I was born on November 3rd, so we always found a day that was good for the both of us, and always used the same method of gifting: we would take something of our own, that was truly dear to us, and gift it to the other.

I always received the most beautiful and appropriate gifts from her! I remember one year when I had a very nice stuffed animal that I was very fond of and I wanted to give it to her. I wrapped it nicely with the most beautiful wrapping paper and ribbon. Then, a few days later, I received an identical stuffed animal as a birthday present from some friends of my sister; yet, they were not aware of our "game of love." The same thing happened with a small ring that I had given her when she was already ill (even though I was very attached to it). For years, I had no idea of whether or not she liked it or what she had done with it. But several years after her departure for Heaven, I met Mamma Teresa who handed me a small box that contained that very ring! My heart almost burst with happiness!

I could go on forever with so many other memories and examples that still fill my heart with emotion and infinite joy. So, Chiara is always present in my daily life. Each morning I begin the day with her, talking to her, entrusting what I'm thinking to her. She's always present, always near.

Laura Terenzani (a friend)

Chiara Luce—smiling and mischievous—stares at me from the photo that's glued to the front page of my diary. And that moment when I'm face to face with her each morning, at the beginning of the workday, is still today the encounter with a friend who encourages me to take a qualitative step, to try to make every moment precious, to try to love every child who walks through the door of my pediatric office, as Chiara knew how to do, with that gaze full of warmth and humanity.

She's an ever-present friend to whom I ask for help when I have to face some thorny situation with my daughters, or if I'm tempted to choose the easy solution when I know that to be Christian means choosing a different one, or if I feel upset for not being able to be as I would have wanted to be.

Chiara Luce's example, despite the unattainable heights that she reached in her earthly life, does not frighten me. On the contrary, it helps me. Her faithfulness in small things enabled her to be faithful in great things; and, starting with the small things, we can all begin again, on any day of any year.

Thank you, Chiara!

Luca Pestarino (a friend)

I met Chiara Luce in Bardonecchia during a Vacation Mariapolis[4] (a summer gathering of the Focolare Movement). On one of the field trips, we had the opportunity to travel much of the route together. We talked a lot about a variety of things. I was immediately struck by her freedom, her freshness, and her precociousness. She

---

4. Mariapolis (City of Mary) is the name given to a summer gathering of the Focolare for people of all ages and backgrounds.

amazed me with how she immediately felt so at ease with someone who was eleven years her senior. She had a beauty that was transparent and fresh, and she was cheerful, always ready with a joke. We laughed and also talked about serious things despite the effort of the climb. That trip marked the beginning of a friendship that also supported her during her illness.

Even though I lived in Genoa, not far from Sassello, my relationship with Chiara was mostly by telephone. Something was keeping me from asking for an appointment to visit her. Only later would I know the reason why.

In 1988, I left for military service. It was a very hard time for me. I was called to live in a way that was consistent with what I believed. However, the easy opportunities for immoral entertainment, cheap drugs, all kinds of abuses, the rush to get high to overcome the frustration of an absurd and alienating experience like the military, required a decision from me to be consistent with what I believed in, and that exposed me to the judgment of many people. In a particularly difficult moment, when for various reasons it had become impossible for me to spend time with the Gen, and the loneliness of facing the daily struggle was even more painful, I decided to telephone Chiara. She already knew something about what I was going through, but this time I wanted to make it clear.

With a calm, sweet, quiet voice, she told me about what she had gone through the day before and how she had offered it all for me. You can imagine how that made me feel. I would have liked to melt into the woodwork with all my little problems, because I wasn't attentive to the fact that I was talking to a girl who was already paralyzed in the blossom of life. The fact is, that's what Chiara was like, always focused on the other person, never turned in on herself or on her own pain and suffering. She made you feel like the most important person on earth, so important that it wouldn't even occur to you to ask what she might be suffering or going through.

Thinking back on this episode many times, I realized something: Despite her young age and the age difference between us, Chiara had become a guide for me and I had been spiritually "cultivated" by her. That's why I didn't dare ask her for an appointment: I never felt up to the task of meeting her, of being at that spiritual level. The roles had reversed themselves, and the younger had become the spiritual mother of the elder. Only saints are capable of such feats.

Ferdinando Garetto (a friend)

Essential, concrete, personal. Chiara gave God with her life, not her words. I met her in the hospital under circumstances that it would take forever to tell. Perhaps we won't ever be able to describe that atmosphere, that presence of Jesus among us during those two years. I remember spending a few minutes in her room and leaving with two impressions: First, how magnificent! A seventeen-year-old who is so sensitive and so strong. The second thought: What will become of that smile when the disease progresses, when she understands her fate? But Chiara never let up. Those of us who had been by her side began to feel that we needed to be inside that room with her, because it was inside her room that we saw the certainty of God's love. There were few words but quite an atmosphere. We felt we had to rise to her level and live for something great. Chiara had taught us throughout her life, even with just her smile and her strong handshake.

Every time, I felt that I had to "fix my soul" before going into her room (more than once I went to confession before going to visit her). But then I would find joy in those brief moments with her. By no merit of my own, I felt projected into an amazing adventure of God's love, often wondering, "Why me?" At the end of our last phone call in September 1990, I remember renewing my unity, in our own way: "One, always!" And Chiara exclaimed with force: "Always!" Now, without being too poetic, I must say that she kept her word: I've "always" felt her with me, day by day: when I met my wife, Mary; in the life of our children and in our family. And, now more than ever, Chiara tells me that "only God can" and only God "matters."

But it's also a great feeling to see how many young people still visit "Chiara's room" and it's the same for every one of them, the same thing that we experienced when we were in that room.

Chiara—it seems to me—made us realize that we only have one life and we *can* live it for something great. But Chiara also tells young people that you don't have to get sick and die in order to become saints. Life itself can be an amazing adventure. You only have to live it well and live it to the fullest, today, moment by moment.

Paola Giribaldi (a friend)

I got to know Chiara in her hospital room. We weren't friends, but we were Gen.

Chiara was one of us, of whom it was asked to give of her life and to continue to love. But she could only do this if we did our small part, if we lived with the same fervor with which she lived, We felt a longing, a duty, to do everything well, which we had never felt before.

During one hospitalization, we learned from Maria Teresa that Chiara was particularly ill. The only contact she had with the outside world was to look at flowers via a mirror that was placed on a back wall, which reflected whatever could be seen from the window. So, we Gen made a big poster with a greeting for her and positioned it in the spot that her mother indicated to us. I'll never forget her satisfaction and her spontaneity. She laughed because the writing appeared backwards in the mirror and she had to "translate" it.

But the last episode is the one that stayed in my heart because it was as if Chiara was passing on the torch to all the Gen. We knew that her condition had greatly worsened. The wish to see her and say goodbye before she left us was really strong, so we went to Sassello.

Maria Teresa had told us that it wouldn't be possible to see her because she was very ill. She was on oxygen and could no longer speak. For us, just being able to pray in that house from downstairs was enough to fully share those hours that were so precious.

As usual, Chiara's mother welcomed us with a hug and a smile, all silent and profound, and gestures that were tender and calibrated, as if everything around us was made of fine crystal. Ruggero, Chiara's aunt, everyone was simply loving. They assured us that as soon as they could, they would let Chiara know that we were there. We prayed the Rosary in a low voice, but with determination. And it seemed to us that every Hail Mary was moving in time with the rhythm of Chiara's breathing, that those Hail Marys were helping her to breathe. We felt one with her.

After a while Maria Teresa came to us wearing a look of surprise and disbelief: Chiara wanted to see us!

Not even Maria Teresa knew how to manage it so that Chiara wouldn't get tired. So together we decided to go up to her and situate ourselves in front of the entrance to her bedroom so that she could see us all standing in the doorframe when the door opened. Our hearts were racing and we were trying to concentrate into one gaze all the things that we would have liked to say to her: that we loved her, that we thanked her for showing us the way, that we understood what she had been trying to tell us with her life, that we would carry on the things she had begun. But she beat us again: As soon as we opened the door she met us with a very sweet smile. She seemed to disappear into the bed. She looked thin and worn, but luminous and essential. Her head was turned toward us and a slender hand moved the oxygen mask so that she could say to us in a whisper, "Have a nice trip." We knew she meant the trip home in the car, but right there in front of us her life spoke of another journey, the journey to God. Then she made a sign with her hand, her thumb clenched in her fist as she raised her hand and said to us,

"One!" We understood that this was a pact she wanted to renew with us, to remain united forever. We answered yes, to count on it, and her gaze entered ours never to go away again.

Orietta Tavaglione (a friend)

One of the last times we met, as always we exchanged some small presents. I don't remember what I brought her, maybe a bunch of wildflowers or some scribbling from my daughter Alice who was a year old, or some fruit juice, which I knew she really enjoyed during that time. But I remember very well what Chiara gave to me: a tiny alarm clock identical to one that she had, and set to the same exact time. Every time I look at it, this gift takes on infinite meanings for me.

Now it's stopped and I can't rewind it, but that's just fine because Chiara is beyond time. And, on the subject of gifts, her last gift [to me] was a red ceramic pot on which she had painted small flowers with our names. When I got back from the ecclesiastical court where I had been summoned to give my testimony, I happened to come across the little pot and felt the urge to pick it up again. I lifted the lid and there underneath—I had never noticed it before!—was written in her handwriting "Thank you!"

Luca Bignone (a friend)

What was Chiara's gift to me? The awareness that everything is perfect just as it is.

I recently found one of my diaries from that time, and here is what I wrote:

Nothing to worry about. Nothing to fear. Nothing to lose. Nothing to overcome.

Nothing to be sorry for. Nothing to be ashamed of. Nothing to cry over.

Nothing to be afraid of. Nothing to conquer. Nothing to escape. Nothing to change.

Nothing to teach. Nothing to hate. Nothing to avoid. Nothing to control.

Nothing to demonstrate. Nothing to force. Nothing to expect. Nothing to judge.

Nothing to refute. Nothing to attack.

Nothing. Only gratitude.

Delfina Nuzzolese Giribaldi
(a friend of the family)

My encounter with Chiara Luce took place at the beginning of 1989, in a small room of the Molinette Hospital in Turin. I had heard about the suspense that Maria Teresa and Ruggero were living in, and I immediately went to the hospital to see if I could make myself useful in some way. Hearing me arrive, Chiara came toward me with a smile. She was tall and very beautiful, with a radiant smile, long dark blond hair tied up with a clip, a light colored pajama, almost like a child. She told me about the surgery she would have to undergo. She was very peaceful, and I left that meeting thinking that the doctors were wrong. There couldn't be any kind of serious illness in such bursting youth! And instead the disease was there!

My husband Vittorio and I realized that she and her family needed a house, so I thought I'd ask our neighbors if they could lend us their empty flat for fifteen days. They're not a practicing family but, because of the relationship of friendship and esteem between us, I allowed myself this request. The answer was an immediate yes, and the two weeks became almost two years, which for me and my family were special because of what Chiara, Maria Teresa and Ruggero gave to us.

There are countless memories from that time. During her chemotherapy, Chiara was hospitalized at the Queen Margherita Hospital. During the day, her mother was at her side and at night her father. Every evening we waited for Maria Theresa to come back and it was always the most precious moment of the day, since she told us the steps that had been taken that day, which were made of so much suffering, but from which we received so much light! Sometimes the chemotherapy treatments were interspersed with a few days of respite, so Chiara and her parents wouldn't go back to Sassello. They would stay in that flat next to ours. In order not to exhaust Chiara, we rarely went into their living space, but we knew that behind that window she was continuing her Holy Journey with her daily offerings of suffering and love.

I remember one special Sunday. Since I was an Extraordinary Minister of the Eucharist, Maria Teresa had asked me to take the Eucharistic Jesus to Chiara who so much desired to receive Him. I couldn't believe that Jesus had given me such a big gift! We recited the Our Father together and Chiara's voice was firm and sweet. When I drew near to offer her the consecrated Host, I had the feeling that I was giving Jesus to Jesus! Chiara's eyes were closed, her hands folded, her body immobilized by the illness! Perhaps all of us in that moment had asked for the miracle, but the miracle was already there, in that tangible experience of Heaven.

Whenever I think about those days, I feel that what Chiara Lubich had once written in a meditation was more than ever true. "I must keep two things secret: love and suffering, because love is the love with which God loves me, and suffering is the love with which I love Him."

Cristina Cuneo (a friend)

There was immediate empathy with Chiara. Our bond became closer after the first hospitalizations. Going to her didn't so much mean to give comfort, but to share together something deeper, moments of joy, of frankness, of wisdom. I sensed that there was a "something more" which I could not put into words, but which attracted me. I remember her understanding glance, her "thank you" when I said to her, "If you need me, I'm here," which was another new beginning in our friendship. We even said the words to each other: "I'm ready to give my life for you," without knowing that that statement would soon become a reality. But even the hardest moments of her illness weren't dark for her—far from it! There was always an air of happiness when we were together. We laughed, sang and shared the small (and large) "daily disasters" that are typical of people in their twenties. The discussions were never trite, but absolutely normal. Like when we talked about the collapse of the Berlin Wall, or the World Youth Day in Santiago de Compostela, or what she was reading, or my graduation thesis. They were simple moments that were made special by that common desire that was born from embracing the charism of Chiara Lubich, to live intensely every moment of the life that God had planned for us.

I remember racing around in order to be able to stop by her room even for just a moment, more often sitting outside the ward with others, on those metal chairs at the hospital, waiting for Maria Teresa and Ruggero to come out to us with their smiles and greetings from Chiara, her news. But I also remember Sassello, her attic, or the lawn of the Badano home with Chiara's aunts and friends, that same lawn where a few years before I shared some special moments with Ruggero who told me about himself and about Chiara. I still sense those shared feelings today whenever I turn to her, renewing the pact which we made in the hospital, entrusting different things to her, both joyful and sorrowful, asking for her intercession or inspiration. And now, as then, the answer is never lacking and still surprises me, creating a bond with her and through her, along with her mother, father and friends, that always gets stronger.

Franz Coriasco (a friend)

I lived Chiara's story from a lateral position, as the brother of her best friend. I underestimated her and sometimes mistreated her. I smiled as you do sometimes with girls whom you consider to be naive. (There were more than ten years between us). But every time our lives crossed, I noted with a certain satisfaction how much she loved me, how much she respected me and considered me an "important" person. Today it's enough to get on the internet to realize who among us would be worthy of that title. But this was only the first of the lessons that Chiara would continue to give me, and she still often does: There are not people nor situations that are more important than others. There is only the responsibility that each of us has for ourself and for the world around us. There is also the power of humility and integrity, the greater usefulness of gesture and respect over words, learning to listen, to live the present moment to the fullest; and the list could go on and on.

I saw her grow and then, with the illness, I saw her shine more and more each day, while I, who had lost the faith, felt like I had been snuffed out. The last time we saw each other, at the end of the existential disasters I was listing for her, she squashed me with an angelic: "Don't worry, Franz, when I'm in Heaven, I will take care of you." And that is practically what happened, even if in ways and in moments I could never have imagined.

In any case, for more than ten years now, Chiara has been much more part of my life than she ever was when she was alive. Not as a memory, but as a presence, and that isn't only because of the books that they've asked me to write about her, or the trips I've taken around the world with my sister and her parents to testify to her extraordinary story. I'm talking about everyday life, about the endless times that I find myself thinking of her, wondering what she would do or suggest in a specific situation, hoping that she will give me a hand when I feel like I can't make it alone. I didn't find my faith in those days, but Chiara continues to be the foot in the door that keeps the door of the faith from completely closing on me. There! That's Chiara for me today, the small glimmer needed to keep hope alive in my heart, the faith for those who don't have it.

Chicca Coriasco (a friend)

Dear Chiara, I would so much like to give you a big hug and share with you all the details of my many challenges, suspenses and secret discoveries. But, to be honest, it's already been a little bit like that over these past years. We made a pact in your little room in August 1990: "The first one who went to Heaven would help the other to get there, and whoever remained on earth would try to fill the great void left by the other." Neither of us ever imagined what the fulfillment of that pact would involve. You're certainly doing the more difficult part now, because to help me go to Heaven you're really going to have to give your all. But for me, that "filling the void" gradually made me realize how big it was.

I would have—indeed I have—a really big desire to hug you again; a knowing gaze would be enough, like the looks we often gave each other, without any need for words in order to perfectly understand each other. And I think it will be like that one day; we'll get lost in this gaze and it won't be necessary to say any words to find one another again, this time, forever.

I saw the heavenly smile of your father right after he departed, which expressed his embrace with you in Heaven.

One day, you entrusted your parents to me, and it was the nicest gift you could have asked of me. We lived so many special moments with them which linked us forever, simple moments, normal but extraordinary because they intimately and indissolubly linked us with you and with Heaven.

Chiara, I have to tell you that you continue to amaze me! You were always able to draw the best out of people who got close to you, and you continue to do so now in a truly amazing and surprising way. How many people have been added to your circle of friends! And you have a personal and exclusive relationship with each one of them. It's absolutely beautiful to see it for myself during the many journeys that you've gifted me with. But each time we leave to go and tell your/our story, or each challenge or choice that pertains to you, there is always a small or large price to pay, because this witness of yours is not a story, but Life that continues still. That's why, today as then, a price must be "paid" so that you can bring all the fruits that your story continues to offer us. That's why I also try to do what I can to get closer to Heaven. Continue to accompany us, as you know how to do, with your little "touches" and your silent presence, that are there, and have always been there. I count on you! Love, Chicca.

The Gen Girls (on the day of Chiara's death)

Chiara, keep us there with you and keep on calling us to follow your path of Light . . . Never leave us, because all of us Gen are relying on you. Hug Jesus, Mary, and all the saints for us. Who knows what a wonderful celebration there will be up there today! You're a beautiful bride, worthy of your Spouse. You have the bridal gown, the bridal bouquet (Did you like it?), a heart full of love, and you're beautiful, infinitely beautiful. Chiara, we love you. Thank you for all your yeses. Thank you for clearing the runway. Let us run like you with our eyes fixed on God-Love and nothing else. Now we are one forever! See you soon! Your Gen.

Chiara Lubich
(Foundress of the Focolare Movement)

I accompanied Chiara with all of you to the Spouse. I thank God for this luminous masterpiece of His and for the edifying testimony of her parents. I ask Him to wrap you all in His infinite love. Your Chiara.

(Telegram from Chiara Lubich sent shortly after the death of Chiara Badano)

> How much light in our Chiara! You can see it on her face, in the photographs of her especially during the last period of her life. How much light in her words, in her letters, in her life that was spent in reaching out to others and loving them so concretely! . . . We can drink of her

life. We can contemplate her life and she can
be a model for us and for all young people, but
also as a witness, for young and old, of an ideal
that had already reached its full maturity in her
at the age of eighteen. . . . In one of her last
letters she confides in me her decision—dic-
tated by nothing but love and the Holy Spirit
in her heart—to love Jesus Forsaken for his
own sake, and not to exploit him for her own
benefit. . . . Chiara knew many pains, especially
during the last stretch of her life on earth. But
she understood that they were precious pearls
that she cherished throughout her days. It was
especially in the suffering required by fortitude,
patience, perseverance and forbearance—all
virtues that any Christian in her situation
would need—that she felt she could love. She
could suddenly recognize and love His Face in
the many surprises, as she called the repeated
alarms from her body as her physical condition
worsened. . . . So, with him she lived, with him
she transformed her own passion into a wedding song. She wanted her body to be dressed
in a bridal gown, seeing to all the details in
advance so that once her soul had passed on to
be "happy with Jesus," as she said everything
would be ready. So she said and so she wanted
her parents to say. Her choice of Jesus Forsaken
was radical, a choice of "what hurts" . . . I invite
all of us to make these words a light for our
path, as a crown for our little saint (as we hope

we will soon call Chiara Luce, or a fulfilled Gen, as our young people would prefer to call her. *What hurts me is mine* more than anything else, just like Chiara Luce. Courage then! Let's not hesitate!

(Worldwide Telephone Link-Up Castel Gandolfo, Italy, March 9, 2000)

Part Four

The Foundation

In Chiara's Name

Several months after the beatification of Chiara Luce, on February 18, 2011, her family and friends founded the Chiara Badano Foundation, which carries her name.

The purpose of the Foundation is to preserve and guard the authentic memory of Chiara Badano and to keep it alive with particular reference to the spirituality that guided her existence; that is, the charism of Chiara Lubich and of the Focolare Movement (also known as "Work of Mary"), in which Chiara Badano was raised and which inspired her for the majority of her life, especially toward the end. Now, she is recognized as one of its brightest and inextinguishable signs and lights.

An added value of this project is the personal experience of the founders and those who contributed to setting up the Foundation, who not only heard about Chiara Luce or read about her, but knew her personally.

As stated in its statutes, the Foundation also has other goals: to support the Petitioner in the Cause of Canonization, Luigi Testore, Bishop of Acqui; to promote the values of fraternity, charity, solidarity, and the growth of mutual love that are inspired by the ideal of unity among individuals and peoples; to support projects that assist the sick and research efforts in the field of oncological pathologies; to support the poorest populations on the continent of Africa. The Foundation is also a main point of reference for the protection of the truthfulness of Chiara's story. Anyone who produces works of any kind concerning the Blessed Chiara Luce is invited to inform the Foundation. The Foundation was established according to a legal model that is not new but relatively atypical: it is a Participation Foundation. It is a non-profit entity, which differs from the traditional definition of a Foundation, characterized by the detachment of the entity from the founders, from an immediately self-sufficient patrimony to the pursuit of the statutory purposes, from the serving position of the administrative body. In fact, the Participation Foundation arises from the initiative of a plurality of founders, each one with a different contribution; it is inspired by the principle of active participation in the management of the institution by all those who intend to offer their contribution and their support. It is characterized as a progressive heritage, that is, open to subsequent growth resulting from new subscriptions, or in any case to forms of superseded support. This open model was chosen in order to share as much as possible the great experience and immeasurable heritage of memories, life, and faith in the unity that the Foundation wishes to express and for which it was established to pursue the ideal of unity that it postulates. The Foundation is a private law institution, not for profit, and cannot distribute profits. It is currently composed of eight founding members chaired by Chiara's mother, Maria Teresa Badano and some of Chiara's friends. There are also the so-called participating members or those—whether they are natural or legal persons, individual or associated, public or private, who share the aims of the Foundation—contribute to its activities and to the achievement of its aims.

As a sign of maximum transparency, each year the Foundation delivers a report to the bishop of Acqui with the relative budget, along with a copy to the Presidency of the Focolare Movement.

The Foundation directly manages the official site dedicated to the Blessed Chiara Badano (www.chiarabadano.org), coordinates the visits of pilgrims to Sassello, requests testimonies, and collects everything that happens in the world regarding Blessed Chiara Badano. Moreover, since 2018, it promotes and administers the annual Chiara Luce Badano Prize, an initiative created to give young people who so desire the opportunity to witness with their own talents how her story, ideals, and lifestyle have fascinated, involved and inspired them. This prize, in which young people between the ages of ten and twenty-five can participate, welcomes different kinds of creative offerings: stories, poems, paintings and sculptures, video clips, dances or mimes, even comics. Each work is evaluated not only for its artistic value, but also for the reasons it was produced.

Finally, among the initiatives that the Foundation has been dreaming of and planning for some time, there is also the creation of a permanent exhibition in Sassello that will present the salient stages in Chiara's life and the spiritual reference points that guided her journey, offering a path that will allow the visitor to know the places of her history and of her beloved Sassello. We are waiting to find the physical location where this can be set up and the funds necessary to begin the work on the realization of something that we know is expected by many. We hope that Chiara and Ruggero will give us a hand with this too.

Acqui Terme, Italy, 17 April 2019
to all the friends of the Blessed Chiara Luce Badano

With this press release we announce the official source of all things concerning Blessed Chiara Badano.

The Chiara Badano Foundation and the Petitioner of the Cause of Canonization, Luigi Testore, Bishop of the Diocese of Acqui, collaborate in full unity, for everything concerning Blessed Chiara Badano.

The previous Postulation has concluded and we are awaiting a new appointment that will carry on the Canonization Process of Chiara Badano. Therefore, the names and references of the previous Postulation are no longer authorized regarding Chiara Badano.

If you are aware of an alleged miracle or a grace received through the intercession of Blessed Chiara Badano, you are asked to send your testimony and any documentation to Curia Vescovile, Piazza Duomo, 9 - 15011 Acqui Terme (AL) - telephone +39 0144.322.078 for the particular attention of the bishop.

We ask that you refer all requests for information and news to the Foundation which can be reached at www. chiarabadano.org.

We ask you, Chiara's friends, to spread as much as possible what the site offers, to give the opportunity to many to be approached and inspired by Chiara's life and informed about the proposals and projects that are collected here.

We ask all Chiara's friends to help to share the website, so that many more people may come to know and be inspired by Chiara's life and be informed about the proposals and projects that are collected here.

The Foundation also desires clarification and transparency in every area, so as to facilitate an official and authoritative direct reference also regarding the law. For the use of Chiara's photos and material, it is required to submit a written request for a written authorization from the Foundation. No marketing in the name of Chiara is authorized. Anyone who collects money in the name of Chiara, for social projects, must obtain written consent. Any important requests will be made known to the bishop. Everything that the previous Postulation had authorized has now expired and its approval must be requested.

We invite you to send to the Foundation all projects and activities that are not yet cataloged under the name of Chiara Luce Badano, so as to include them in the map at www.chiarabadano.org.

It is a constant source of joy to see the Life that continues to grow around Chiara's memory, the Light that brings fruits of testimonies and new projects. We would like to gather and share it through the website. This work is also useful for the Canonization Process.

The Chiara Badano Foundation has its office in Sassello, Italy, and was established, by the express will of the parents of Blessed Chiara Luce Badano, Ruggero and Maria Teresa, on February 18, 2011, with an act of the Notary Luisa Quaglino Rinaudo from Turin, Italy. The current President of the Foundation is Chiara Badano's mother. The Foundation was established with the aim of preserving and reserving an authentic living memory of Blessed Chiara Badano, with particular reference to the spirituality of which she was a luminous sign, with due regard to the ideals and purposes of the Work of Mary-Focolare Movement, which Blessed Chiara Luce Badano totally embraced and made her own and was inspired by during her earthly life.

The primary commitment of the Chiara Badano Foundation is and always will be the continuous and direct collaboration with the Plaintiff of the Cause of Canonization in the Diocese of Acqui, as this letter confirms.

We sincerely hope that this press release will clarify and illuminate every reality that concerns Blessed Chiara Luce Badano, bringing to order the peculiarities that others, in the past, have attributed to themselves in a personal and improper manner and without title; so that Chiara's style and her message can be as clear and true as she was and the direct link with the Foundation, made up of witnesses, can further promote the spreading of her story and the great spiritual depth that characterized it.

Chiara herself will help us, as she has always done, in this important task.

Luigi Testore, Bishop of Acqui

Maria Teresa Caviglia, The President
of the Chiara Badano Foundation

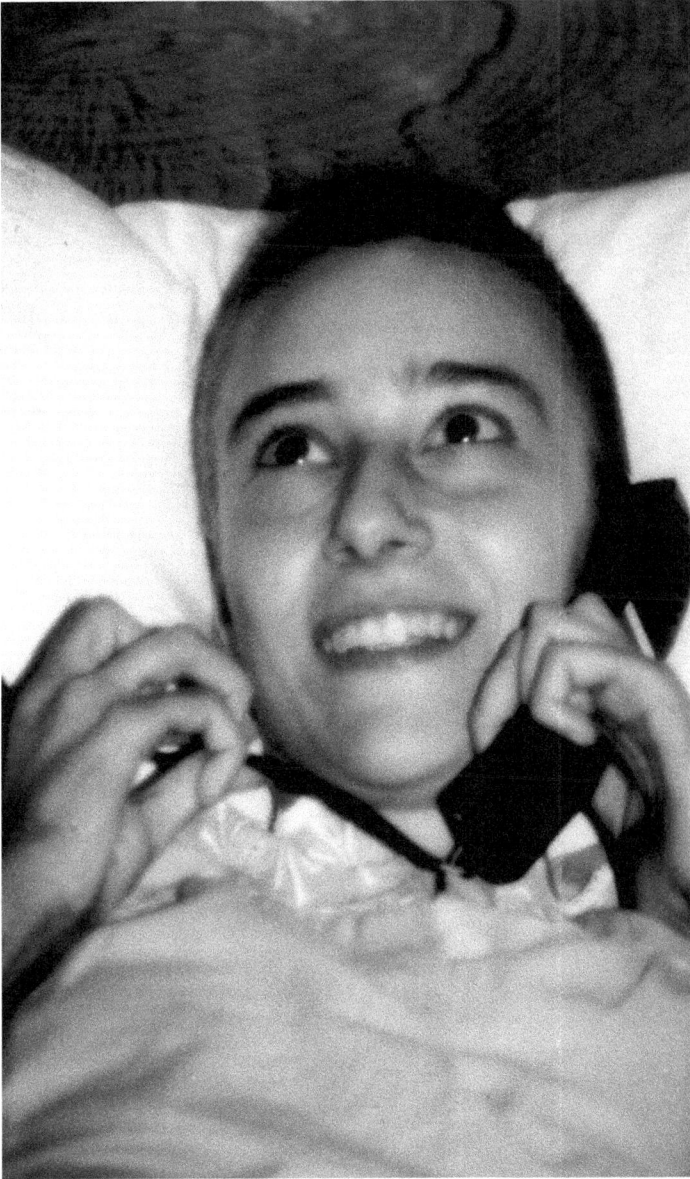

In order to sustain the projects and purposes of the Chiara Badano Foundation please contact:

fondazione@chiarabadano.org
www.chiarabadano.org
C.F. 92094240097 - IBaN
It26X0335901600100000019687